Behold, God's Son!

D1246574

CHRISTOPH CARDINAL SCHÖNBORN

Behold, God's Son!

Reflections on the Gospel during the Year of Mark

Translated by Henry Taylor

IGNATIUS PRESS   SAN FRANCISCO

Title of the German original: *Seht, Gottes Sohn! Gedanken
zum Evangelium im Markusjahr*
© 2005 by Molden Verlag, Vienna

Cover art:
This painting of the Crucifixion, which hangs in the
diocesan administrative offices of the archbishop's palace
in Vienna, was attacked and defaced by the Hitler Youth
who stormed the palace on October 8, 1938

Author's photograph:
© KronenZeitung / Martin A. Jöchl

ISBN-13: 978-1-58617-177-3
ISBN-10: 1-58617-177-1
Library of Congress Control Number 2006936321
Printed in the United States of America ⊗

CONTENTS

Lent and the Easter Season

Feasts in the Church Year

INTRODUCTION

Thanks to the Second Vatican Council (1962–1965), the Gospel readings in Sunday worship are spread out, not just over one year—as had for centuries been the case—but over three years. That has given us the chance to hear far more extracts from the Gospels than we could in only one year. Thus, as the Council intended, "the treasures of the Bible" are being "opened up" (Constitution on the Liturgy 51). The current three "lectionary years" are each centered on one of the "synoptic" Gospels: Matthew, Mark, and Luke. The passages from the Gospel of John are spread over all three years.

After having the opportunity to expound the Sundays and feasts of the "Year of Matthew", in *My Jesus: Encountering Christ in the Gospel* (San Francisco: Ignatius Press, 2005), I am happy to be able to offer here brief commentaries for lectionary year B, the "Year of Mark". I hope soon to be able to explain the Gospels of the "Year of Luke", in a third book.

Each of the four evangelists has his own, quite unmistakable shape. All four are talking about Jesus. All four witness to their belief in him as the longed-for Messiah of Israel, the Son of God. The Master whom they love and revere, whose words and deeds they accurately pass on to us, is unmistakably one and the same. Yet it is nonetheless true that the evangelists themselves—their temperaments, their way of believing, and their personal faith story—leave their mark on the picture they draw of Jesus. They are not thereby distorting the picture of Jesus, but they do cast light on him from different sides.

Who was Mark? And what does he emphasize? According to an old tradition, he is supposed to have come from Jerusalem. His mother was called Mary. The first Christian congregation used to meet at her house for prayer and worship (cf. Acts 12:1–17). We find Mark as the companion of Barnabas in the first "mission team" led by Paul. And thereby "there arose a sharp contention" between Paul and Barnabas concerning him. This conflict even led the two great missionary apostles to separate for a while. Barnabas took Mark with him to his homeland of Cyprus, to carry on the mission there (Acts 15:36–40).

There was certainly a reconciliation later. Mark became a faithful assistant and brother to Paul, in prison in Rome. And Peter, too—already in Rome by that time, like Paul—calls Mark "my son" (1 Pet 5:13).

So we are not surprised that later tradition sees Mark as Peter's "interpreter", carefully writing down whatever he heard about Jesus from Peter. According to tradition, Peter sent Mark to Egypt, where he became "chief shepherd", the first bishop of the new Christian community.

Did Mark know Christ personally? Probably, at least at the end, when he was taken prisoner and suffered his Passion (cf. Mk 14:51f.). He certainly belonged to the milieu of the first congregation in Jerusalem. I wonder whether his picture of Jesus is not strongly influenced by Peter. For no other evangelist talks about Jesus in such a "human" way as he does. Anger and sorrow, Jesus' passionate emotional responses, are more clearly mentioned in Mark than in the other Gospels.

However human Jesus may appear here, it is Mark in particular who also strongly emphasizes his divinity. The climax of the whole Gospel is the witness of the Roman centurion, a pagan, looking at Jesus, who has died on the Cross: "Truly this man was the Son of God!" (Mk 15:39).

Everything Mark tells us about Jesus is intended to lead us to the same confession of faith as made by this soldier, who was in charge of putting Jesus to death in this agonizing way. Through his Gospel, Mark intends to bring about what he himself experienced with Paul and with Peter: that through stories about Jesus, people come to believe in him.

Belief is what the Gospel is about; it is not simply a biography of an interesting person. The first of Jesus' sayings that Mark reports is an urgent challenge to believe: "The time is fulfilled, and the kingdom of God is at hand; repent, and believe in the gospel" (Mk 1:15).

Changing the way we think, changing our way of life and converting, that is what the Gospel is about. The new way that Jesus shows us is not wide and comfortable. It demands our assent to our own cross. It costs a lot, but it gives us much more. Giving up the old way and walking in this new way is a good bargain.

Before I dispatch to my readers the following simple attempts to help people read the Gospel, I should add a word of thanks. Thanks above all to the *Kronen Zeitung* newspaper. Sunday by Sunday, it makes a page available for me to comment on the Gospel of that day. Most of the pieces in this book first appeared there, while some commentaries have been added, for the sake of completeness. I am grateful to my kind colleagues on the editorial team of the "Krone" and, likewise, to my faithful assistants in the Archdiocese of Vienna, Frau Maria Faber, Herr Andreas Gutenbrunner, Frau Christine Mitter, and Frau Ingrid Cech, who type out my manuscripts (I still prefer to write with my fountain pen) and illustrate them, as also to Professor Erich Leitenberger, who often helps when my pieces are too long. Finally, my thanks to Dr. Hubert Philipp Weber, who through his persevering and faithful collaboration is jointly responsible for publishing this book.

This book is dedicated to the founder of the *Kronen Zeitung*, Hans Dichand. In the face of a great deal of criticism of his newspaper, there are three traits I appreciate and admire in him: he is a brilliant newspaper editor; at critical junctures he has always intervened in a statesmanlike manner for the general good; even in the most difficult periods, he has never given in to the trend of cheap and frequently unjustified criticism of the Church. My thanks to him for all this, as for his generous support of so many good causes. *Ad multos annos*—a long life!

Vienna, Feast of the Exaltation of the Holy Cross
September 14, 2005

Advent

and

the Christmas Season

The Gospel of Mark 13:24–37

[*Jesus said to his disciples:*] *"In those days, after that tribulation, the sun will be darkened, and the moon will not give its light, and the stars will be falling from heaven, and the powers in the heavens will be shaken. And then they will see the Son of man coming in clouds with great power and glory. And then he will send out the angels, and gather his elect from the four winds, from the ends of the earth to the ends of heaven.*

"From the fig tree learn its lesson: as soon as its branch becomes tender and puts forth its leaves, you know that summer is near. So also, when you see these things taking place, you know that he is near, at the very gates. Truly, I say to you, this generation will not pass away before all these things take place. Heaven and earth will pass away, but my words will not pass away.

"But of that day or that hour no one knows, not even the angels in heaven, nor the Son, but only the Father. Take heed, watch and pray; for you do not know when the time will come. It is like a man going on a journey, when he leaves home and puts his servants in charge, each with his work, and commands the doorkeeper to be on the watch. Watch therefore—for you do not know when the master of the house will come, in the evening, or at midnight, or at cockcrow, or in the morning—lest he come suddenly and find you asleep. And what I say to you I say to all: Watch."

৵

A Successful Advent

Advent begins with the same message with which the old Church year ended: "Watch!" The Church's year begins on the First Sunday of Advent.

Advent means coming. The season of Advent is a time of waiting for someone who is to come. Christians are waiting for the coming of Christ.

That is something they have in common with the Jewish people, who are also waiting and hoping that the Messiah (the "Anointed", called the *Christos* in Greek) will come. Christians believe that the Messiah has already come—Jesus of Nazareth. That is why Advent leads up to the feast of Christmas, the celebration of the birth of Jesus.

But Christians are also waiting for the Second Coming of Christ, his coming again "with great power and glory", as Jesus himself promised (Mk 13:26).

When this will happen, we do not know; we cannot calculate the time of it; we can only wait vigilantly for it. That is what unites Christians with the Jewish people: both are waiting for the Messiah, for his glorious and liberating coming. The Jews believe that his name is still unknown; Christians believe that Jesus, the Christ and Son of God, will one day come again. Both Jews and Christians, however, share in waiting hopefully.

The little parable Jesus tells in today's Gospel also talks about waiting: The man who stands at the door, the doorkeeper or porter, has to wait until the master comes home. And since the boss has not said exactly when he is coming home, the doorkeeper has to stay awake until he comes, even if it is not until midnight or toward morning. Waiting requires us to be alert. Anyone waiting for a green traffic-light watches it carefully, so as to be able to drive off straightaway.

On an assembly line, people always have to watch carefully to ensure that all the procedures are correctly carried out. Anyone waiting at home for a guest to arrive has his ears pricked to hear the doorbell.

The life we live today demands a great deal of alertness from most people. On the roads, even a few seconds' inattention may have fatal consequences. Thus, Jesus' demand is nothing new for us: Look out!

Yet Jesus means to say more than merely: Look out on the roads and when using technology. It is above all a matter of looking out for our neighbor. It is lovely to meet people who look out for others, who are able to pay attention to others, who can feel what is moving them, what they need.

Being alert as we go through life requires keeping our eyes open, with our heart at the ready, not just centered on ourselves and not just seeing ourselves. Only that kind of alert living is really exciting and enriching.

Advent is meant to make us alert. It is amazing how many people, during these weeks, go to the so-called Rorate Masses early in the morning. It does us good to meet together to watch and pray, early in the day.

Advent reminds us of the first coming of Jesus, as a child at Bethlehem, and of his Second Coming at the end of time. Yet between the two there is another, third coming of Jesus: whenever he knocks at the door of my life today, quietly and without great show, whenever he wants to come to me unexpectedly—am I awake, then, or does he find me sleeping? This silent coming may take place at any time: through some person who needs me; through prayer, when God speaks to my heart; through an illness striking me down; through some happy event that I dimly feel is a gift from God. Being on the lookout for this day-by-day coming of God, that is having a successful Advent.

The Gospel of Mark 1:1–8

The beginning of the gospel of Jesus Christ, the Son of God.

As it is written in Isaiah the prophet,
"Behold, I send my messenger before your face,
who shall prepare your way;
the voice of one crying in the wilderness:
Prepare the way of the Lord,
Make his paths straight—"

John the Baptist appeared in the wilderness, preaching a baptism of repentance for the forgiveness of sins. And there went out to him all the country of Judea, and all the people of Jerusalem; and they were baptized by him in the river Jordan, confessing their sins. Now John was clothed with camel's hair, and had a leather belt around his waist, and ate locusts and wild honey. And he preached, saying, "After me comes he who is mightier than I, the thong of whose sandals I am not worthy to stoop down and untie. I have baptized you with water; but he will baptize you with the Holy Spirit."

෫෨

The Origin of the Beginning

What was at the beginning? How did everything begin? All four evangelists start with a glance at the origin of the "good news", at the beginnings of Jesus and his Church.

20

The evangelist Matthew starts with a genealogy of Jesus, which runs back through David to Abraham, the patriarch. Jesus is the fruit of the long story of God's dealings with Abraham and his descendants.

Saint Luke opens his Gospel with a historical prologue. He dedicates his work about all "the things which have been accomplished among us" (Lk 1:1) to a Christian benefactor whose name is Theophilus, to whom he intends to demonstrate how reliable the reports about these events are and that he can rely on their trustworthiness.

The Gospel of John begins with the famous prologue, which illuminates the most profound and mysterious origins of the events involving Jesus recounted in the Gospel: "In the beginning was the Word, and the Word was with God, and the Word was God" (Jn 1:1). Here, the "beginning" is the inmost mystery of the life of God himself, the origin of all origins, the origin with no beginning, within God himself, which in the language of Christianity we call the mystery of the Holy Trinity. John contemplates how everything comes forth from this original spring: creation, life, light, and above all the eternal Word, which has become human and become flesh, the Son of God, Jesus Christ the Messiah, from whom we have received "grace upon grace" (Jn 1:16)

The shortest prologue is that of the shortest of the four Gospels. Saint Mark was the pupil and companion of the Apostle Peter and (as an old tradition tells us) his translator in Rome; he was also the Apostle Paul's companion and assistant on his missions and was in serious conflict with him for a while, but in Rome, when Paul was in prison, he gave him faithful support. Above all, Mark is said to have faithfully reproduced what the Apostle Peter preached. His Gospel is brief and recounts not so much Jesus' words as his deeds. He depicts Jesus vividly, often with strong emotional reactions. That, it seems to me, accurately reflects the Apostle Peter's temperament.

Mark prefaces his Gospel with only one brief sentence. Yet how pregnant each word is! "The beginning of the gospel"—that can mean simply: the beginning of the book we have in our hands. Yet John also talks about the "beginning", as do the first words of the Bible: "In the beginning God created the heavens and the earth" (Gen 1:1).

Here, "The beginning" means, not merely the chronological start, but also the origin. The Gospel comes from the deepest wellspring, from within the living God himself. It is his life-giving message, which is directed to all men, so that all may have life, and "have it abundantly".

The divine origin of the good news has come close to us. He has a name: Jesus himself is the "place" in which the origin is present. That is why the Gospel is trying to achieve one thing, above all: to bring the reader to believe in Jesus. Through believing, through faith, we have access to the original source, which is available to us in Jesus.

Two steps of faith are requisite for this: confessing that Jesus is the Messiah, the Christ for whom Israel is waiting. At the midpoint of Mark's Gospel, Peter articulates this confession of faith: "You are the Christ" (Mk 8:29). When the Gospel closes, face to face with the man who has died on the Cross, the Roman centurion takes the second step: "Truly this man was the Son of God!" (Mk 15:39).

It is to this dual confession of faith, which the first sentence of the Gospel expresses in anticipation, that the listeners and readers are meant to be led. John the Baptist, who prepares the way for the Lord Jesus Christ, makes his appearance as the first witness to this. We see the apostles as the last witnesses, as they go forth into all the world to proclaim the gospel. In doing so, they are not departing from the beginning, for Christ, the enduring origin of the gospel, accompanies and supports their mission—right up to today!

THIRD SUNDAY OF ADVENT

The Gospel of John 1:6–8, 19–28

There was a man sent from God, whose name was John. He came for testimony, to bear witness to the light, that all might believe through him. He was not the light, but came to bear witness to the light. . . .

And this is the testimony of John, when the Jews sent priests and Levites from Jerusalem to ask him, "Who are you?" He confessed, he did not deny, but confessed, "I am not the Christ." And they asked him, "What then? Are you Elijah?" He said, "I am not." "Are you the prophet?" And he answered, "No." They said to him then, "Who are you? Let us have an answer for those who sent us. What do you say about yourself?" He said, "I am the voice of one crying in the wilderness, 'Make straight the way of the Lord,' as the prophet Isaiah said."

Now they had been sent from the Pharisees. They asked him, "Then why are you baptizing, if you are neither the Christ, nor Elijah, nor the prophet?" John answered them, "I baptize with water; but among you stands one whom you do not know, even he who comes after me, the thong of whose sandal I am not worthy to untie." This took place in Bethany beyond the Jordan, where John was baptizing.

෴

John, Who Prepares the Way

Gaunt, with a kind of animal skin as his garment, a staff in one hand and the other outstretched, pointing to Jesus: that is how artists portray him. John is his name, John the Baptist.

It is with him that we are concerned today. Who was he? This question was put to him by the religious authorities in Jerusalem: "Who are you?" His parents were called Zechariah and Elizabeth. His father was a Jewish priest, his mother was a relative of Mary of Nazareth, who was to become the mother of Jesus. Elizabeth was barren, and it was rightly seen as a miracle when very late in life she nonetheless bore a child: John. We know nothing further about his childhood, only that he went out into the wilderness at an early age, probably to the people who at that time were living in a kind of monastery beside the Dead Sea, like the Essenes. A monastery like this has been excavated at Qumran, where the famous scrolls were also found.

Around A.D. 30, John began to preach and to call people to penitence, and many came to hear him. Those who were willing to convert, he plunged into the Jordan, as a sign of purification and of a new beginning. The fact that so many people came made the authorities in Jerusalem suspicious. They got nervous, for the political and social climate was heated and full of tensions. Many people were waiting for something to happen, for someone to come and free Jerusalem and Israel from the hated Roman yoke.

The question was hanging in the air: Is this John, in the wilderness beside the Jordan, the saving Messiah?

"I am not he!" John rejects all the speculation. What are you up to, then? "I am the voice of one crying in the wilderness, 'Make straight the way of the Lord.'"

Even today, we say of someone who courageously admonishes or warns people that he is "a voice in the wilderness".

That is John's "calling". He does not have himself in mind; he is trying to prepare the way. "I have been sent before him" (Jn 3:28), he says at one point, in respect of Jesus. And on the same occasion he also utters this great saying, "He must increase, but I must decrease" (Jn 3:30).

John is a person who entirely effaces himself. He is called the forerunner, and thus he understands his ministry as entirely preliminary and provisional. The people who come to him are not supposed to cling to him but to find their way to faith in Jesus Christ.

As a man, John is a marvelous example. He does not set himself at the center of things; he wants to be a helper, an intermediary, someone who prepares the way, a companion for people on their way. Anyone can take something of this attitude from him.

As a believer, John is a marvelous example. He is trying to be a voice completely reliant on God and on his representative, Jesus Christ. He does not stand in God's way but shows people the way to God. He is happy if he can help other people come to faith. Each one of us can only take this attitude as our yardstick with gratitude and wonder: "Prepare the way of the Lord!"

The Gospel of Luke 1:26–38

In the sixth month the angel Gabriel was sent from God to a city of Galilee named Nazareth, to a virgin betrothed to a man whose name was Joseph, of the house of David; and the virgin's name was Mary. And he came to her and said, "Hail, full of grace, the Lord is with you!" But she was greatly troubled at the saying, and considered in her mind what sort of greeting this might be. And the angel said to her, "Do not be afraid, Mary, for you have found favor with God. And behold, you will conceive in your womb and bear a son, and you shall call his name Jesus.

> *He will be great, and will be called the Son of the Most High;*
> *and the Lord God will give to him the throne of his father David,*
> *and he will reign over the house of Jacob for ever;*
> *and of his kingdom there will be no end."*

And Mary said to the angel, "How can this be, since I have no husband?" And the angel said to her,

> *"The Holy Spirit will come upon you,*
> *and the power of the Most High will overshadow you;*
> *therefore the child to be born will be called holy,*
> *the Son of God.*

And behold, your kinswoman Elizabeth in her old age has also conceived a son; and this is the sixth month with her who was called barren. For with God nothing will be impossible." And Mary said, "Behold, I am the handmaid of

the Lord; let it be to me according to your word." And the
angel departed from her.

How Can This Be?

The Gospel of the Annunciation is among the best known of all. The scene can be found in countless paintings, as the angel Gabriel brings Mary the news that she is going to conceive a child who will be called "Son of the Most High", thus, Son of God, and that he will reign forever as king. Mostly, the artists have tried to portray Mary's fright. Ancient tradition says that Luke, who wrote the account of this scene, was not only a doctor but also an artist. In any case, he had a great gift for depicting events in very concrete fashion.

But where does Luke get his knowledge? Is his story reliable? Is it credible at all for a child to be supposedly not procreated by a man but conceived by the Holy Spirit?

Luke himself says that he has "followed all things closely", so that the reader "may know the truth concerning the things of which you have been informed" (Lk 1:3–4). I think only one person could have been a reliable witness for Luke at this point: Mary herself. Only she witnessed the scene with the angel. Only she knew that the child she had conceived, and to whom she had given birth, was not that of any man but had been given her in a marvelous way by God. Only she could talk about that, and I assume that she did so to people who already believed in their hearts that Jesus, her son, was really the Son of God.

There were enough people who mocked, even in Nazareth, who spread rumors that Mary's child had not been begotten by Joseph—for they had not lain together at all, as yet—but was the result of an indiscretion committed with a Roman soldier named Pantera. This gossip had a long life and was also widely repeated in polemical writings against the Christians.

Mary herself asks, "How can this be, since I have no husband?" And she receives the answer, "With God nothing will be impossible." And then she experiences in her own body how what is humanly impossible is possible for God: she becomes a mother; she is expecting a baby and believes that it is God's Son she is carrying in her womb. When she brings him into the world, in poverty, in Bethlehem, she firmly believes that in that silent, holy night she has given birth to the Savior, the Redeemer.

But no one would have believed her about all that unless many other people had had experiences that were at least similar: the shepherds from the fields in the neighborhood, the Wise Men who came from far off in the East, and later the many people who met Jesus, her son, and who encountered his power to heal, his understanding, his love, and who for their own part came to believe this: "You are the Christ, the Son of the Living God."

There are still people today who celebrate with gratitude, at Christmas, the fact that God really came to us as a man— through Mary.

CHRISTMAS DAY

The Gospel of Luke 2:1–14

In those days a decree went out from Caesar Augustus that all the world should be enrolled. This was the first enrollment, when Quirinius was governor of Syria. And all went to be enrolled, each to his own city. And Joseph also went up from Galilee, from the city of Nazareth, to Judea, to the city of David, which is called Bethlehem, because he was of the house and lineage of David, to be enrolled with Mary his betrothed, who was with child. And while they were there, the time came for her to be delivered. And she gave birth to her first-born son and wrapped him in swaddling cloths, and laid him in a manger, because there was no place for them in the inn.

And in that region there were shepherds out in the field, keeping watch over their flock by night. And an angel of the Lord appeared to them, and the glory of the Lord shone around them, and they were filled with fear. And the angel said to them, "Be not afraid; for behold, I bring you good news of a great joy which will come to all the people; for to you is born this day in the city of David a Savior, who is Christ the Lord. And this will be a sign for you: you will find a baby wrapped in swaddling cloths and lying in a manger." And suddenly there was with the angel a multitude of the heavenly host praising God and saying,

"Glory to God in the highest,
and on earth peace among men with whom he is
pleased!"

Becoming like a Child!

What a contrast! The great emperor Augustus, the most powerful man of that age, the ruler of the enormous Roman Empire, gives an order, and everyone has to obey. Throughout his empire, people have to get themselves enrolled in the tax registers, so that sufficient taxes may flow in from every part of the empire, taxes the emperor needs to finance his empire, to sustain and expand his military power, to lay down the marvelous network of roads to all parts of the Roman Empire, and to construct the great palaces, theaters, baths, and stadiums.

How trivial, in comparison, is what happens to this little family from Nazareth, who set out to obey the imperial command and to have themselves enrolled in the tax registers in Joseph's hometown, in Bethlehem. They are so insignificant that there is no imperial palace at their disposal, not even a place in the local inn. They have to make do with a stall for the mother to give birth.

Today, we are celebrating, not the emperor Augustus, but that birth in the stall at Bethlehem. For this child, shortly before he is crucified, will say to the representative of the Roman emperor, the governor Pontius Pilate, "You would have no power . . . unless it had been given you from above" (Jn 19:11).

It is not the emperor who is lord of the world, but the child in the crib. The names of the emperors, like those of the other great men of this world, have long passed away and been forgotten; yet everywhere on earth, the birth of this child is still celebrated.

What an angel declared then to the poor shepherds in the fields near Bethlehem is still true: "I bring you good news of a great joy . . . for to you is born this day . . . a Savior, . . . the Lord." The words "this day" still hold good.

Ever since this child was born, he has not ceased to demonstrate his rule: not with tanks, like those that stand in Bethlehem today, but with his message, which was sung by the angels in the night of poverty in which he was born: "Glory to God in the highest, and on earth peace among men with whom he is pleased." Against all appearances, the power of love is still greater than that of weapons, and the peacemakers are the ones to be praised, not the men of violence.

In Bethlehem, in the Holy Land, war is dominant even today, and the weapons are louder than the Christmas carols. Has the birth of the child who is God's Son and who is to reconcile men to God not brought the promised peace?

Yet even then, peace seemed like a distant dream. And yet, at that time, people found peace with this child: first the shepherds and, then, the Wise Men from the East. Thus it has remained to this day: only those who, as Jesus says, themselves "become like a child" can and will find peace beside the crib of the divine child and, then, themselves give peace to others.

———

The Gospel of Luke 2:22–40

And when the time came for their purification according to the law of Moses, [the parents of Jesus] brought him up to Jerusalem to present him to the Lord (as it is written in the law of the Lord, "Every male that opens the womb shall be called holy to the Lord") and to offer a sacrifice according to what is said in the law of the Lord, "a pair of turtledoves, or two young pigeons." Now there was a man in Jerusalem, whose name was Simeon, and this man was righteous and devout, looking for the consolation of Israel, and the Holy Spirit was upon him. And it had been revealed to him by the Holy Spirit that he should not see death before he had seen the Lord's Christ. And inspired by the Spirit he came into the temple; and when the parents brought in the child Jesus, to do for him according to the custom of the law, he took him up in his arms and blessed God and said,

"Lord, now let your servant depart in peace,
according to your word;
for my eyes have seen your salvation
which you have prepared in the presence of all peoples,
a light for revelation to the Gentiles,
and for glory to your people Israel."

And his father and his mother marveled at what was said about him; and Simeon blessed them and said to Mary his mother,

"Behold, this child is set for the fall and rising
of many in Israel,

and for a sign that is spoken against
(and a sword will pierce through your own soul also),
that thoughts out of many hearts may be revealed."

And there was a prophetess, Anna, the daughter of
Phanuel, of the tribe of Asher; she was of a great age,
having lived with her husband seven years from her virgin-
ity, and as a widow till she was eighty-four. She did not
depart from the temple, worshiping with fasting and prayer
night and day. And coming up at that very hour she gave
thanks to God, and spoke of him to all who were looking
for the redemption of Jerusalem.

And when they had performed everything according to
the law of the Lord, they returned into Galilee, to their
own city, Nazareth. And the child grew and became
strong, filled with wisdom; and the favor of God was upon
him.

৯

What Will Become of the Child?

Whenever I baptize a child, I am always stirred by the question, "What will become of you? What will your life look
like?" And even more for the parents, joy is mingled with
questioning: the joy over the newborn child, the questions
about how things will probably go for him in this world.

The Presentation of Jesus in the temple by his parents,
forty days after his birth, arouses similar feelings. Mary comes
to offer the sacrifice of purification prescribed, for herself
and for her successful delivery. Jesus, the firstborn, is to be
dedicated to God in accordance with the law of Moses, since
every firstborn creature belongs to God.

This is a moving scene: the aged Simeon takes the child in his arms. He, who is already standing on the threshold of death, greets the newborn child: here is a picture of rejoicing over the budding of new life and of a grateful farewell to this life. Simeon, that righteous, upright man, thus became a symbol of the evening of life. His song of thanks—"Lord, now let your servant depart in peace"—has therefore become the one, in the prayer of the Church, that is sung or prayed just before going to bed.

Yet his is a particular joy: by divine inspiration, he recognizes, in this little child of poor people, the longed-for and promised Messiah of the Lord, who is to bring light and salvation to all peoples. The ancient widow Anna, who also comes along, has a similar experience and recognizes how enormously important this child will be one day.

In the joy of this meeting of old and young, of farewell and a new beginning, are also mingled solemn tones. Simeon can see in advance that this child will encounter a great deal of opposition. It is in their encounter with him that one spirit will be distinguished from another. He will become a stumbling block for many, a sign of contradiction. It will hit his mother hard, when her child meets with such enmity. Sorrow will pierce her heart like a sword.

With these joyful, yet alarming, words in their hearts, Mary and Joseph return to Nazareth (the evangelist Luke does not tell us about the intervening flight into Egypt). There follow long years of secluded life, maybe thirty years: daily life, work, nothing unusual, making a living as a carpenter, cares and happiness . . . Mary carries in her heart what Simeon said about the child and her. What will become of her son, Jesus, who is growing up, becoming a young man, an adult? Mary believes and trusts. It certainly was not easy, having this feeling that something difficult was waiting for him and her. Yet when she was standing beside the Cross and her son was dying in agony, then she once more gave her assent, as she had before to the angel.

SOLEMNITY OF MARY THE MOTHER OF GOD

The Gospel of Luke 2:16–21

And [the shepherds] went with haste, and found Mary and Joseph, and the baby lying in a manger. And when they saw it they made known the saying which had been told them concerning this child; and all who heard it wondered at what the shepherds told them. But Mary kept all these things, pondering them in her heart. And the shepherds returned, glorifying and praising God for all they had heard and seen, as it had been told them.

And at the end of eight days, when he was circumcised, he was called Jesus, the name given by the angel before he was conceived in the womb.

ૐ

Time for Reflection

Simple shepherds were the first witnesses of the events that took place at Bethlehem. To this day, it is the simple folk who are ready to go out and see what God is doing on earth.

What happened to them? That night they were keeping watch by their flocks, as on many previous nights, to protect them from thieves and predators. Then they saw a shining figure, a messenger from God, who said to them, "To you is born this day in the city of David [Bethlehem] a Savior, who is Christ the Lord" (Lk 2:11). And he told them how they would know where to find him: "a baby . . . lying in a manger" (Lk 2:12).

Is all that a pious legend, without any substantial truth? It helps me to think about comparable events in our own time. In Fatima, the great place of pilgrimage in Portugal, everything began in the year 1917 with three children minding goats. They, too, saw an angel, then apparitions of Mary; they heard messages and were entrusted with tasks they had to fulfill. Today, millions of people go on pilgrimage to Fatima to find consolation, help, and strength. Many other examples could be mentioned, down the centuries, since Bethlehem.

What is common to them all is that heaven has something to say to us. And mostly it is simple, straightforward people, especially children, who are open to hearing it. And, like many pilgrims in our own day, the shepherds then set out to see the place of grace they had heard about.

What they found was nothing unusual: simply a mother, Mary, who had only just given birth, Joseph, and the newborn child—all of them in great poverty, in a stable, with the child lying in the manger.

Nonetheless, the shepherds greatly rejoiced. I think their joy must have been of the kind that is experienced even today in holy places. This comes, not from any kind of sensational experience, but from finding for oneself that heaven is open here and that God's presence can be felt. Many people discover this quite particular and special joy at places such as Lourdes, Fatima, or Medjugorje.

And then the story was told. The shepherds told people about what had happened to them; and the people whom the shepherds told about it talked about it to others. And thus the news of the marvelous event at Bethlehem was spread abroad. Up to this day, things are no different. And every time, there is great joy when heaven comes really close to the earth.

Mary, however, stored up all these things in her heart and reflected on them. Luke, the evangelist, emphasizes that as an example for his readers. Christmas is soon past. All the New Year celebrations, and then we are into the new year. Where is the time really to weigh up, in our hearts, what happened at Christmas? If we hurry from one event to another, then nothing can take root in the depths of our heart. Thinking about God's coming in my own life and reflecting on it, like Mary: that would be a good resolution for a blessed New Year.

The Gospel of John 1:1–5, 9–14

In the beginning was the Word, and the Word was with God, and the Word was God. He was in the beginning with God; all things were made through him, and without him was not anything made that was made. In him was life, and the life was the light of men. The light shines in the darkness, and the darkness has not overcome it. . . .

The true light that enlightens every man was coming into the world. He was in the world, and the world was made through him, yet the world knew him not. He came to his own home, and his own people received him not. But to all who received him, who believed in his name, he gave power to become children of God; who were born, not of blood nor of the will of the flesh nor of the will of man, but of God.

And the Word became flesh and dwelt among us, full of grace and truth; we have beheld his glory, glory as of the only-begotten Son from the Father.

A Trail of Light Leading Home

The first words of the Bible are, "In the beginning God created the heavens and the earth" (Gen 1:1). Then follows, in solemn, poetic words, the account of the work of creating everything: light and darkness, sun, moon, and stars, earth, land and sea, plants, animals, and finally men—God's creation.

The Gospel of John has an opening that sounds similar: "In the beginning . . ."—it is not the creation that follows, however, but what was there before that: "In the beginning was the Word." And then follows—again in solemn, poetic words—who "the Word" is and what he does and achieves.

But why it is that these words from the beginning of the Gospel of John are heard on the Second Sunday after Christmas becomes clear from the last verse: "And the Word became flesh and dwelt among us." These mysterious words are talking about the child in the manger. They tell who this newborn child really is: a human child, but not only that. His origins go back farther and deeper than our own. We are people begotten of men, but Jesus is "God from God", as the Nicene Creed says. He is God's Son, who has become man, has taken on "flesh", our mortal humanity, who has become one of us.

God became man: that is what we say about the Christ Child in the manger. Yet can God become man, then? That is what today's Gospel is talking about. God is never alone. He is neither silent, at a loss for a word, nor is he dull, lacking in spirit: his Word and his Spirit are with him. God is community: Father, Son, and Holy Spirit.

And because it is his will that many should share in his community, he created everything "through the Word". Everything—really everything! For there is nothing, in all the whole universe, from the greatest thing to the least, that has come there "of itself"—certainly not life. All life comes from God, and most certainly human life, endowed with understanding and a will. And all light in human life springs from this one divine source: every good thought, every insight and perception, and all good will come "from the Word" of God, from God's presence in every human life. Every ray of light in my life can lead me back to the divine source of light if I follow it.

The pity is that we prefer darkness to the light, time and again, and do not follow God's trail of light. That is why God brought his light right into our midst, why his Word became flesh, why God became man. In the Christ Child, in Jesus Christ, God speaks his Word in human language, comprehensible to anyone who is seeking, a joy for anyone who finds it, so that no one has to wander about lost, so that all of us may find our way home as God's children.

EPIPHANY OF THE LORD

The Gospel of Matthew 2:1–12

Now when Jesus was born in Bethlehem of Judea in the days of Herod the king, behold, Wise Men from the East came to Jerusalem, saying, "Where is he who has been born king of the Jews? For we have seen his star in the East, and have come to worship him." When Herod the king heard this, he was troubled, and all Jerusalem with him; and assembling all the chief priests and scribes of the people, he inquired of them where the Christ was to be born. They told him, "In Bethlehem of Judea; for so it is written by the prophet:

'And you, O Bethlehem, in the land of Judah,
are by no means least among the rulers of Judah;
for from you shall come a ruler
who will govern my people Israel.'"

Then Herod summoned the Wise Men secretly and ascertained from them what time the star appeared; and he sent them to Bethlehem, saying, "Go and search diligently for the child, and when you have found him bring me word, that I too may come and worship him." When they had heard the king they went their way; and behold, the star which they had seen in the East went before them, till it came to rest over the place where the child was. When they saw the star, they rejoiced exceedingly with great joy; and going into the house they saw the child with Mary his mother, and they fell down and worshiped him. Then, opening their treasures, they offered him gifts, gold and frankincense and myrrh. And being warned in a dream not

43

to return to Herod, they departed to their own country by another way.

વ

What Gives Me Hope

The astrologers from the East were pagans, but that does not mean they were godless. They had an extraordinary knowledge of heavenly phenomena. In those days, in the East, there was such an exact knowledge of astronomy, such precise calculations, that we can only be amazed. Yet these scientists of the time did not merely know their way around the heavens; they never made a separation between science and religion. The universe spoke to them of God and his activity. I wonder whether we, today, with all our knowledge about nature, are able to read God's language and his handwriting? Can we let ourselves be addressed by natural phenomena, either small or mighty ones, and can we grasp what God has to say to us in them?

Another thing that makes me think is the way that the Wise Men from the East set out to find the person concerning whom the particular constellations and conjunctions of stars spoke to them. We, too, meet with great signs—natural catastrophes, for instance. Would we take the trouble to look for the person about whom these events have something to say to us?

The meaning of suffering is not always immediately clear. The pain is too great for that. Yet how moving it is to meet with a trust that God is to be found in all this suffering. Here is something we can learn from these astrologers, as also from people who are affected by catastrophes of that kind—looking for God in our lives.

A third idea occurs to me: Herod, "and all Jerusalem with him", was frightened by what the Wise Men from the East said. God's coming to earth as a child frightens powerful people.

Herod, the tyrant who was drunk with power, who had exterminated half his family because of fears for his power (three sons, his wife, his brother-in-law, and his mother-in-law), feared nothing so much as he feared any disturbance of the existing balance of power, even if this came from God, bringing salvation and hope to mankind.

The great catastrophes of our own day have given rise to a worldwide attitude of solidarity, and from this a great hope has sprung up among those directly affected.

It concerns me when I see how comfortable people are with this. Will the people in power understand the sign that God has given them? Will all this help from all over the world really give new hope to the countries affected? Will party interests, and those of power and economics, bury this hope again?

To end with a sure and certain hope: the Wise Men did not let themselves be deterred by Herod. They found the newborn King of peace, Christ the child, and Mary, his mother.

Even today there will be some wise men like that. No difficulty, no power games or selfishness will prevent them from finding Christ in the victims of catastrophes and bringing to them the gifts of love and solidarity. I am filled with confidence that, even today, love will be stronger than any catastrophes and stronger than all human mistakes!

The Gospel of Mark 1:7–11

And [John the Baptist appeared in the wilderness and] preached, saying, "After me comes he who is mightier than I, the thong of whose sandals I am not worthy to stoop down and untie. I have baptized you with water; but he will baptize you with the Holy Spirit."

In those days Jesus came from Nazareth of Galilee and was baptized by John in the Jordan. And when he came up out of the water, immediately he saw the heavens opened and the Spirit descending upon him like a dove; and a voice came from heaven, "You are my beloved Son; with you I am well pleased."

Through the Year with Mark

Mark is going to accompany us throughout the year with his Gospel. His is the shortest Gospel. An old tradition says that Mark wrote it in Rome, on the basis of the memories and the preaching of Peter the Apostle, who was crucified in the emperor Nero's circus in A.D. 67, along with many other Christians, precisely where the Basilica of Saint Peter now stands in the Vatican.

Mark's mother, whose name was Mary, had a house in Jerusalem where the first Christians liked to meet (cf. Acts 12:12). On his first missionary journey, Paul took the young Mark along as a companion, though of course he soon went

46

back home "to mother". That is why, later, there was a heated dispute about him—there already were heated disputes in the early Church—and Paul chose another companion, named Silas, while Mark went on mission to Cyprus with Barnabas until finally he became Peter's colleague in Rome.

The style of Mark's Gospel is terse and spare, paying more attention to Jesus' actions than to his preaching. Mark is not afraid to give expression to Jesus' feelings, his occasional "holy wrath", his sorrow, the urgency he feels to the point of being impatient. At the same time, Jesus' divinity breaks through quite clearly in Mark, time and again. The one who seems so human to us is also indivisibly "the Son of God", as the very first verse of the Gospel says.

Mark tells us nothing about the childhood of Jesus. He starts with Jesus' baptism in the Jordan. With this event, Jesus stepped out of his hidden life into the light of public life. What moved him to take this surprising step of having himself baptized? John the Baptist was calling people to conversion and penitence. The external sign of this was immersion in the water of the Jordan, an act and a symbol of cleansing. John was trying to prepare people for the coming of the Messiah. They were to change their lives and to be on the alert for the coming of the great time of renewal. He called the coming Savior someone "mightier than I" and saw himself as merely his servant.

John's surprise must have been all the greater when quite unexpectedly Jesus appeared among the people who came to John to receive the baptism of repentance. The great one whose coming John had proclaimed came humbly and quietly, like one sinner among others. What did it mean? John received an answer "from heaven". God gave us to understand that Jesus' attitude was pleasing to him, that in doing this Jesus was showing himself to be God's "beloved Son".

What does Jesus' first public appearance have to say to us? Two things: I should prepare the way for the coming of God in my life. To that end, many hindrances on my path need first to be cleared away, many crooked things made straight. What is still more important, however, is that God himself comes down to me, that he shows no aversion to me, to my failings or my mistakes. In that baptism in the Jordan, he took my guilt upon his shoulders. That is why it is not permissible for anyone who wishes to find God to exalt himself above other people or to look down on them. God finds anyone who steps down as Jesus did. That is what meets with God's approval, not self-satisfied pride.

Ordinary Time

———

The Gospel of John 1:35–42

John was standing with two of his disciples; and he looked at Jesus as he walked, and said, "Behold, the Lamb of God!" The two disciples heard him say this, and they followed Jesus. Jesus turned, and saw them following, and said to them, "What do you seek?" And they said to him, "Rabbi" (which means Teacher), "where are you staying?" He said to them, "Come and see." They came and saw where he was staying; and they stayed with him that day, for it was about the tenth hour. One of the two who heard John speak, and followed him, was Andrew, Simon Peter's brother. He first found his brother Simon, and said to him, "We have found the Messiah" (which means Christ). He brought him to Jesus. Jesus looked at him, and said, "So you are Simon the son of John? You shall be called Cephas" (which means Peter).

෨

The First Meeting

It stayed in his memory, unforgettable: his first meeting with Jesus. He knew the exact time of day: it was about four in the afternoon ("about the tenth hour"). John was probably writing this as an old man, and the memory of it was as fresh as when it first happened. For this meeting was decisive for his whole life. There was a clear "before" and "after" about it.

What happened in these first hours spent with Jesus gave a whole new direction to his life. But let us see how this came about.

Next Sunday we will read how Mark, who is going to stay with us throughout the year with his Gospel, depicts the calling of Jesus' first followers. Among them was John. In his own Gospel he does not say anything about this calling, but he does recount his very first meeting with Jesus. That is even more important to him; it is, so to speak, one of the secrets of his heart.

John, a fisherman by trade, as was Andrew, belonged to the group of disciples around John the Baptist. Fascinated by this ascetic's convincing lifestyle and by his teaching, which spoke directly to them, they had joined up with the Baptist to take part in his "school of life". The Baptist, however, had always made it clear to them that he was only preparing the way for someone else and that he would not want to stand in that person's way. So he let them both go when they followed Jesus so as to know more about him.

"What do you seek?"—"Where are you staying?"

Those were the first words that passed between them. Nothing exciting, and yet they were unforgettable, because it was he who had looked at them and spoken to them and who from then on was the center of their lives; everything turned on him.

So they went with him and saw where he was staying and spent the rest of the day with him. Strange, that there is not one word about what they saw or what they talked about. This is all the more surprising, since John gives a fuller account than the other evangelists of Jesus' conversations and speeches.

This first meeting remained his own secret. It was so precious to him that he kept it to himself. Yet his experience and that of Andrew, during those few hours, must have been quite decisive. For the next day, Andrew said to his brother Simon, whom Jesus would thereafter call Cephas, Peter, which means "rock": "We have found the Messiah!"

This expresses all the enthusiasm and the joy springing from that first meeting.

John and Andrew had found the one for whom many of their people had been waiting. Andrew then did what is the most natural thing to do when anyone has been granted a meeting of decisive importance: he wants other people to share in this. So he took his brother Simon to see Jesus. And meeting Jesus was decisive for his whole life, too.

To finish, three questions: Has there been a comparable moment of meeting in my own life? With another person? With God? With Jesus? Do I remember it? Was this a turning point in my life? And did I tell other people about it, take other people to experience the same meeting?

It would fill many books if everyone were to tell us about his first meeting.

The Gospel of Mark 1:14–20

Now after John was arrested, Jesus came into Galilee, preaching the gospel of God, and saying, "The time is fulfilled, and the kingdom of God is at hand; repent, and believe in the gospel."

And passing along by the Sea of Galilee, he saw Simon and Andrew the brother of Simon casting a net in the sea; for they were fishermen. And Jesus said to them, "Follow me and I will make you become fishers of men." And immediately they left their nets and followed him. And going on a little farther, he saw James the son of Zebedee and John his brother, who were in their boat mending the nets. And immediately he called them; and they left their father Zebedee in the boat with the hired servants, and followed him.

ॐ

Come! Behind Me!

Dark clouds overshadow the beginning. John the Baptist has been thrown into prison. The tyrannical King Herod could not bear John when he was preaching repentance, saying to him, "It is not lawful for you to have your brother's wife" (Mk 6:18). Anyone who voices unpalatable truths has to reckon with unpleasant results. Against this background, Jesus begins his public ministry in his native Galilee. His path, too, will end with prison and the Cross.

At the start, however, there is a cry that brings hope: "The kingdom of God is at hand!" The kingdom of God—that was a phrase filled with hope: God is finally going to produce just circumstances and bring about an age of peace. An end to oppression, terror, and war! Many people were longing and hoping for this time. But Jesus makes it clear that God's good kingdom will not come unless we cooperate. It is not great political upheavals that will bring it about, but the conversion and faith of individuals. Changing our own lives, putting our bad habits behind us, repenting of our own mistakes and being ready to do penance for them: without these steps, which no one can take for us, God's age of peace will never reach us.

Yet turning away from old wrongs is only one side of it. The other, positive side is a renewed turning to God. Jesus calls this "believing": "Believe in the good news." The kingdom of God, peace, and righteousness come when we trust anew in God.

What that might look like in practice is shown by the two scenes of "calling" that follow here. Two pairs of brothers, fishermen by trade, whom Jesus simply calls, briefly, succinctly, conclusively, to go along with him. "Come! Behind me!" (That is what he says, literally.) He does not explain much; he neither tells them what the rate of pay is nor arranges for insurance and holidays. They put their trust in him; they leave everything—occupation, family, environment—and go with him, following behind him into an utterly uncertain future. Such complete trust astounds us. Was this not behaving frivolously and irresponsibly toward their own families?

Countless other people have since responded to a call from Jesus in the same way these first four did. They have often had to put up with people saying to them, "How can you let your parents down like that?" "How can you leave your job like that?" "Where's the common sense in that, what has that to do with any rational plan?" Yet without this trust in Jesus and his call, someone like Francis (1181–1226) would never have left his father's business; someone like Mother Teresa would never have left everything in order to be with dying people in Calcutta.

Is that true only of "special" callings like those of priests and religious? I do not think so. For changing one's life, rethinking it all and being converted, believing anew in God and trusting in him, is not limited to only a few. There are times in everyone's life when a new start of that kind is called for. Then it is a matter of leaving behind what is familiar, and that can be very painful. But if I know who is calling me to do this and whom I can trust in doing it, then this is a step toward a new life.

The Gospel of Mark 1:21–28

And they went into Capernaum; and immediately on the sabbath [Jesus] entered the synagogue and taught. And they were astonished at his teaching, for he taught them as one who had authority, and not as the scribes. And immediately there was in their synagogue a man with an unclean spirit; and he cried out, "What have you to do with us, Jesus of Nazareth? Have you come to destroy us? I know who you are, the Holy One of God." But Jesus rebuked him, saying, "Be silent, and come out of him!" And the unclean spirit, convulsing him and crying with a loud voice, came out of him. And they were all amazed, so that they questioned among themselves, saying, "What is this? A new teaching! With authority he commands even the unclean spirits, and they obey him." And at once his fame spread everywhere throughout all the surrounding region of Galilee.

৵

The First Day of the New Creation

The evangelist Mark presents Jesus to us by depicting the events of the first day of his public ministry in Capernaum. He concentrates the most important messages about Jesus, Jesus' whole program, so to speak, as if at a focal point, in this first beginning.

In Matthew's Gospel, it is the Sermon on the Mount, the essence of Jesus' message, that is placed at the beginning.

In Luke's Gospel, everything starts with Jesus' "first sermon" in the synagogue of his hometown, Nazareth, when he explains his public appearance by the light of Old Testament prophecy.

Mark does not, in the beginning, talk about the content of Jesus' preaching. He does not say anything yet about the teaching that Jesus proclaims. He is interested in the effect that he has. Right from the start, it is the person of Jesus that has the center stage: he himself is the message. He is the new thing that has arrived, the beginning and the origin of a reconstituted world.

We can see two clear signs of this in what happens on that first day of public ministry in the synagogue at Capernaum (the remains of which can still be seen).

First, the effect his words have. They must have been incomparably powerful. Many people witness to that. What was it, in particular, about the way he spoke, about his sermon? Mark describes people's response: he does not teach the way learned people, "scholars", do; rather, he teaches like someone who has "authority".

It was not his oratory that was powerful. People do not say, "Doesn't he speak beautifully!" Rather, they are "struck". His words strike home. They are effective. He does not offer opinions, interesting contributions for discussion, but "teaches on authority, as the person with ultimate responsibility, with complete validity" (K. Stock).

No man can say about his own words what Jesus says about himself at one point: "Heaven and earth will pass away, but my words will not pass away" (Mk 13:31).

Our words may be helpful or damaging, may build up or destroy. But only he can create something new with his word.

Jesus' words have the same power as the words of the Creator, when he said, "Let there be . . ."—and it was so.

Jesus gives the first demonstration of the power of his word right at the start of his ministry. Someone who is possessed starts to cry out. It is not he who is yelling, but the demon within him. He "senses" who Jesus is and where the power that people can feel is coming from: "I know who you are, the Holy One of God." One word from Jesus is enough, and the person possessed is free, liberated from the bonds of the demon.

This scene may seem strange to us, but it should not. We have recently seen drawing to its close a century that has shown the naked power of evil as hardly any century in the past has done. Auschwitz and the Gulag Archipelago are names that represent great eruptions of evil.

From the first day onward, Jesus stands up against this power, and the power is against him. The Evil One (Jesus quite openly calls him "Satan" [Mk 3:23] and "a murderer from the beginning" [Jn 8:44]) sees in Jesus' coming the end of his rule. Freeing people from his power is Jesus' mission, what his task is. Have this mission and task failed? How could there have been a Hitler and a Stalin? Has Jesus been vanquished in the struggle with evil?

Often, it really looks like that. But look with the eyes of faith! What do you see? He has still set a limit to evil, from that first day in Capernaum, right up to today.

FIFTH SUNDAY IN ORDINARY TIME

The Gospel of Mark 1:29–39

And immediately [Jesus] entered the house of Simon and Andrew, with James and John. Now Simon's mother-in-law lay sick with a fever, and immediately they told him of her. And he came and took her by the hand and lifted her up, and the fever left her; and she served them.

That evening, at sundown, they brought to him all who were sick or possessed with demons. And the whole city was gathered together about the door. And he healed many who were sick with various diseases, and cast out many demons; and he would not permit the demons to speak, because they knew him.

And in the morning, a great while before day, he rose and went out to a lonely place, and there he prayed. And Simon and those who were with him followed him, and they found him and said to him, "Every one is searching for you." And he said to them, "Let us go on to the next towns, that I may preach there also; for that is why I came out." And he went throughout all Galilee, preaching in their synagogues and casting out demons.

Come into My Home!

Anyone who has ever been in Capernaum will listen to this Gospel with particular attention. The old fishing village on the shore of Lake Gennesaret has been rediscovered by archaeological digging, and nowadays it is a popular destination for pilgrims. This is where Jesus stayed, after he left his home village of Nazareth to start on his new work: bringing the message of the imminent kingdom of God among men. This was where Simon Peter and his brother Andrew lived, the men whom Jesus called to set out on the road with him.

Among the excavations at Capernaum, the remains of the beautiful synagogue stand out. Jesus preached in that synagogue. This is where he healed the sick and freed the possessed through exorcism. Here, he spoke those unforgettable words about the "Bread from heaven", which he himself is, and that he would give people his flesh to eat: the Eucharist.

It makes a deep impression when you read these extracts from the Gospels there, in the very place where they happened. If you leave the synagogue, you can follow a short path between the remains of houses to where, according to an old tradition, Peter's house stood; today a modern church has been built over the place, but it still leaves open to view the remains of Peter's house.

Why am I telling you this? Because the Gospel is not telling a fairy tale, but recounting a story that really happened, at that place and that time. The excavations in the Holy Land are a strong and trustworthy witness to these events. That is why, from time immemorial, so many people have wanted to go on pilgrimage to the Holy Land, to tread upon the ground on which Jesus walked. In Capernaum, you can see today's Gospel vividly before your eyes.

The day we are being told about was a sabbath. That is why everyone went to worship in the synagogue. Only Peter's mother-in-law was unable to go. We know through this passage that Peter was married. The story that Jesus could heal the sick had soon gone around. The sabbath, with its obligatory sabbath rest, was hardly over when, just after sunset, people were streaming together and bringing to the front door all kinds of sick people and people who were possessed.

But Jesus did not take the way of success; the very next day, he left, first for silence and prayer, then to carry on his work in other towns and villages. Why should he not come as far as us, right into the places we live, into our homes? He said that he had come, at that time, to go first to Galilee and then, after his death and Resurrection, into all the world, to all men. Thus, this Gospel story can happen where we live; Jesus can come into my home, and "take by the hand and lift up" me or one of my loved ones, whoever particularly needs it. We need only to trust and to ask it of him, as Simon Peter did then on his mother-in-law's behalf.

The Gospel of Mark 1:40-45

And a leper came to [Jesus] begging him, and kneeling said to him, "If you will, you can make me clean." Moved with pity, he stretched out his hand and touched him, and said to him, "I will; be clean." And immediately the leprosy left him, and he was made clean. And he sternly charged him, and sent him away at once, and said to him, "See that you say nothing to any one; but go, show yourself to the priest, and offer for your cleansing what Moses commanded, for a proof to the people." But he went out and began to talk freely about it, and to spread the news, so that Jesus could no longer openly enter a town, but was out in the country; and people came to him from every quarter.

੭≈

I Will—Be Clean!

I can see them in front of me—the dozens of lepers along the side of a highway in Nigeria. An unforgettable and dreadful sight: old and young, with their faces and limbs eaten away by leprosy. The cars were speeding past; no one stopped. They have their leprosy clinics, after all, our driver said. Leprosy can be cured nowadays, if the appropriate drugs and the requisite level of hygiene are available. There are many places in the world where these are both still lacking. Yet many people are helping to make treatment and cure available for these poorest people. I knew one of them, a Dominican father, an elderly American, who had lived with the lepers for forty years in the Philippines, both beloved and revered, helping in quite selfless fashion, a man of the gospel.

In Jesus' time, people suffering from leprosy were totally excluded. They were not allowed to touch anyone and lived outside the villages; if anyone came near them, unaware, they had to call out and warn them, "Unclean! Unclean!" Touching them was strictly forbidden, and if you did so, you made yourself "unclean" thereby. People's fear of those suffering from AIDS in our own day recalls this a little.

Jesus obviously did not share those fears. He let the leper come up to him, he did not run away or drive the leper away. On the contrary, he touched him, moved to pity. Even before Jesus had physically healed him, the thing that is more important had happened: someone who had been thrust out of society felt he was a person again.

Here was someone who saw in him, not the danger, the threat of uncleanness, but a human brother, along with whom he was suffering, whose feelings he shared.

The example Jesus gave has been effective. Saint Francis of Assisi (1181–1226), who overcame his own feelings and embraced a horribly disfigured leper, is the best-known instance. There have been countless other people, up to this day, who have not turned away from someone else's suffering, who have continued to see their disfigured neighbor as a person, as a brother or sister, and who have thus helped someone not to despair at his own misery.

Yet there is more: the leper had heard of Jesus, heard about his healings. He had a strong new hope that drove him to Jesus: "You can make me clean, if you are only willing to!" He was not disappointed in his trust: the miracle, the inconceivable thing, did happen: he was completely healed.

The step of trusting is decisive. The Bible calls that "believing". Do I believe that Jesus can heal my leprosy? My inner wounds, my burden of sin, or my torment of conscience? Everything that, like leprosy, cuts me off from others and destroys my self-respect, gradually bringing me death? Do I really believe, as this leper did, that Jesus can heal me completely?

One day, if I dare to take the step of going to Jesus, kneeling down before him and simply bringing all my afflictions to him, then he will say to me, too, "I will—be clean!"

SEVENTH SUNDAY IN ORDINARY TIME

The Gospel of Mark 2:1–12

When [Jesus] returned to Capernaum after some days, it was reported that he was at home. And many were gathered together, so that there was no longer room for them, not even about the door; and he was preaching the word to them. And they came, bringing to him a paralytic carried by four men. And when they could not get near him because of the crowd, they removed the roof above him; and when they had made an opening, they let down the pallet on which the paralytic lay. And when Jesus saw their faith, he said to the paralytic, "Child, your sins are forgiven." Now some of the scribes were sitting there, questioning in their hearts, "Why does this man speak like this? It is blasphemy! Who can forgive sins but God alone?" And immediately Jesus, perceiving in his spirit that they questioned like this within themselves, said to them, "Why do you question like this in your hearts? Which is easier, to say to the paralytic, 'Your sins are forgiven,' or to say, 'Rise, take up your pallet and walk'? But that you may know that the Son of man has authority on earth to forgive sins"—he said to the paralytic—"I say to you, rise, take up your pallet and go home." And he rose, and immediately took up the pallet and went out before them all; so that they were all amazed and glorified God, saying, "We never saw anything like this!"

❧

The Power to Forgive

Just imagine it: suddenly someone breaks in through the ceiling, and through the hole that is made a stretcher is lowered down, straight to Jesus' feet, with people pressing close all around him because they want to see him and hear him. Even with the flimsy way in which houses were built in those days, it was a most unusual thing to do.

The four men who bring the paralyzed man to Jesus in this imaginative way must have considerable determination and will not be deterred by any obstacle. And they are doing this, not for themselves, but for someone else who could no longer do things for himself.

Jesus is unmoved by the quite shameless way these men force themselves upon him, and he does not make a fuss about the fact that they have damaged his house in forcing an entry (how would I react, if someone tried to get into my house that way?). He is interested in something else: the unshakeable belief the four of them have that Jesus can help their paralyzed friend. Whether the friend himself believes that makes no difference. It is their firm faith that impresses Jesus. Does that not mean that we can bring other people before God in faith? What else are we doing whenever we pray for a friend who is ill? In doing so, we express our confidence that Jesus can help that person.

And when we do that, our prayer should be just as importunate as those men who took the roof up. How many parents have brought their children to him in prayer like that (and how many children have done it for their parents!). Yet why does Jesus say to the paralyzed man, "Your sins are forgiven"?

To us, it is the bodily paralysis that seems to be the great evil. For Jesus, sin is by far the greater evil. What really oppresses man, what cripples him in life, is above all his refusal of God, distancing himself from him, which we call "sin". We cannot escape by our own efforts from this paralysis of our vital powers. No forgetting or repressing of it, no psychological methods, however good they may be, can heal this. Only God can take from us the crippling burden of sin.

Jesus' opponents also know that, and they say, "Who can forgive sins but God alone?" No man can do it—no doctor, no therapist, even I myself cannot forgive my sins. I can only push them aside, repress them, but that does not heal me. But Jesus can forgive my sins because he is not merely a man; he is the Son of God.

What those four big strong men do with one paralyzed man, Jesus has done for all men: he has taken upon himself the burden of our sins; he has broken down the walls of death and has made it possible for us to live a new life, reconciled with God.

I love this Gospel, and I hear it as though Jesus were saying to me, today, "My son, your sins are forgiven. Stand up, walk again, be joyful and lively once more!"

The Gospel of Mark 2:18-22

Now John's disciples and the Pharisees were fasting; and people came and said to [Jesus], "Why do John's disciples and the disciples of the Pharisees fast, but your disciples do not fast?" And Jesus said to them, "Can the wedding guests fast while the bridegroom is with them? As long as they have the bridegroom with them, they cannot fast. The days will come, when the bridegroom is taken away from them, and then they will fast in that day. No one sews a piece of unshrunk cloth on an old garment; if he does, the patch tears away from it, the new from the old, and a worse tear is made. And no one puts new wine into old wineskins; if he does, the wine will burst the skins, and the wine is lost, and so are the skins; but new wine is for fresh skins."

৯৯

A Joyful Fast

Jesus' Jewish hearers must have been shocked when the scene in today's Gospel was enacted before them. In those days, fasting was a sign of practicing religion in ordinary life. Many people fasted twice a week, on Monday and Thursday—something that lived on in Catholic tradition, in which Wednesday and Friday were fast days. For a long time, you could recognize a Catholic because he ate no meat on Friday, just as Jews and Moslems do not eat pork. Fasting was seen as a religious practice, not as a way of keeping slim. Setting perceptible limits to one's eating was seen as a penance for one's sins and a way to free oneself from one's desires. In short, fasting was something pious.

That is exactly what Jesus did not do, and his disciples followed their Master's example. Was Jesus irreligious? "A glutton and a drunkard" (cf. Mt 11:19), those were the names he was called by some strict believers. He had of course practiced quite radical fasting himself, when he was alone in the wilderness for forty days. It was not as a joke or because he was irreligious that he was not fasting now. He gave a quite different reason for it, one that must really have shocked the people who heard him: When a wedding is being celebrated, then you simply cannot fast.

Jesus called himself the bridegroom. That was unheard of. For in those days, every Jew knew that the prophets of old had repeatedly described God as the bridegroom and the Jewish people as the bride. The famous Song of Songs, in the Old Testament, sang of this love in passionate and erotic imagery. God and his people—a long, exciting, and often painful love story!

And that was precisely what Jesus applied to himself. He was the bridegroom. He was putting himself in the place of God. Rejoicing is appropriate now: It is a wedding celebration, and that is when you celebrate, not fast! Incredible presumption, thought those critics who heard him: "You, being a man, make yourself God" (Jn 10:33).

Yet Jesus went a bit farther than this. He announced that there would be a time when he would be "taken away" from his disciples. He would be killed, he would no longer be visibly here among us. Then it would be time to fast again, time for penance and for cutting down on things. That is why

70

there is a time of fasting even for Christians: Lent, beginning on Ash Wednesday.

But this is a particular kind of fasting. Jesus wanted people to fast joyfully, not with woeful faces displayed to public view. For all those who set out along the way with Jesus, it is always a wedding celebration, because he has promised that he is always with us—a constant reason to be joyful. That is why it is possible for joy to be the keynote of the Christian life. But we have not yet reached our goal. Unfortunately, we may still lose our way and fail to get there. That is why we have to be alert, in order to avoid becoming careless and inattentive. And that is where fasting and praying can help. This is quite as true today as it was then.

The Gospel of Mark 2:23–3:6

One sabbath [Jesus] was going through the grainfields; and as they made their way his disciples began to pluck heads of grain. And the Pharisees said to him, "Look, why are they doing what is not lawful on the sabbath?" And he said to them, "Have you never read what David did, when he was in need and was hungry, he and those who were with him: how he entered the house of God, when Abia-thar was high priest, and ate the showbread, which it is not lawful for any but the priests to eat, and also gave it to those who were with him?" And he said to them, "The sabbath was made for man, not man for the sabbath; so the Son of man is lord even of the sabbath."

Again he entered the synagogue, and a man was there who had a withered hand. And they watched him, to see whether he would heal him on the sabbath, so that they might accuse him. And he said to the man who had the withered hand, "Come here." And he said to them, "Is it lawful on the sabbath to do good or to do harm, to save life or to kill?" But they were silent. And he looked around at them with anger, grieved at their hardness of heart, and said to the man, "Stretch out your hand." He stretched it out, and his hand was restored. The Pharisees went out, and immediately held counsel with the Herodians against him, how to destroy him.

૬>

What Is Becoming of Sunday?

"Observe the sabbath day, to keep it holy, as the LORD your God commanded you. Six days you shall labor, and do all your work; but the seventh day is a sabbath to the LORD your God; in it you shall not do any work." That is what it says in today's Old Testament lesson from the "fifth book of Moses", Deuteronomy (5:12–14).

To this day, the sabbath rule is the commandment that is most frequently discussed in Judaism. In the state of Israel, it leads to complicated practical questions in everyday life: Can buses run on the sabbath? And can airplanes fly? How do you cook on a sabbath, if kindling a fire counts as work and that is forbidden? And does that equally apply to an electric current? Switching it off—does that count as work? When does it, and when not?

As long ago as Jesus' time, there was much discussion among Jews about the sabbath laws. Jesus took part in these debates.

There is a good deal of work people have to do on the sabbath: giving drink to domestic animals, for instance. And it is permissible to save life; indeed, we have to do so, when someone is in danger. That is work that does not breach the sabbath.

Are these not simply over-scrupulous discussions? Beware of prejudices! It is right that the sabbath should be holy, for as believing Jews tell us, man does not live for his work alone. He was not created for the day-to-day treadmill. The goal of human life is to rest with God. Work is a necessary means for living. And the sabbath is not there just so that we may gather our strength again for everyday life, as a built-in break, so to speak, for the machinery of work.

"The sabbath was made for man", says Jesus. That is why Judaism struggles so hard to ensure that this seventh day is kept free from all servitude for man. Slaves, too—indeed, even beasts of burden—are not allowed to work on the sabbath.

Yet in Jesus' eyes, Judaism had certainly made the sabbath rules much too over-scrupulous. Thus a danger arises that the liberating significance of the sabbath may become covered over with the wasteland of laws and rules. Today's Gospel gives two examples of this.

Plucking ears of corn in the fields, on the sabbath of all days? Jesus defends his disciples, since they are really hungry. (Can we still imagine what that is like?) In Jesus' company, they are miserably poor. Should they not be allowed to satisfy their hunger a little, then? And the man with the withered hand: Is Jesus not allowed to do good on the holy day of divine rest by healing a poor sick person?

So then they decide to have Jesus killed. Through blind zeal, something that is good—the sabbath rest—has become hostile to man. Jesus is filled with anger and sadness at their rigidity and hardness of heart.

Today, too, we should be sad and angry if Sunday is coming to be increasingly dominated by the mechanisms of economic "pressures". We are far from the Jews' strict rules about sabbath rest. The Sunday custom of rest from work is being breached more and more often. Man, whom God intends to rest on a free day so that he may remain human, is out of business.

The Gospel of Mark 3:20–35

Then [Jesus] went home; and the crowd came together again, so that they could not even eat. And when his friends heard it, they went out to seize him, for they said, "He is beside himself." And the scribes who came down from Jerusalem said, "He is possessed by Beelzebul, and by the prince of demons he casts out the demons." And he called them to him, and said to them in parables, "How can Satan cast out Satan? If a kingdom is divided against itself, that kingdom cannot stand. And if a house is divided against itself, that house will not be able to stand. And if Satan has risen up against himself and is divided, he cannot stand, but is coming to an end. But no one can enter a strong man's house and plunder his goods, unless he first binds the strong man; then indeed he may plunder his house.

"Truly, I say to you, all sins will be forgiven the sons of men, and whatever blasphemies they utter; but whoever blasphemes against the Holy Spirit never has forgiveness, but is guilty of an eternal sin"—for they had said, "He has an unclean spirit."

And his mother and his brethren came; and standing outside they sent to him and called him. And a crowd was sitting about him; and they said to him, "Your mother and your brethren are outside, asking for you." And he replied, "Who are my mother and my brethren?" And looking around on those who sat about him, he said, "Here are my mother and my brethren! Whoever does the will of God is my brother, and sister, and mother."

Jesus—Stumbling Block

The Church is often an obstacle and an offense. Time and again her "human side", the mistakes and sins of her members, brings many people simply to reject the Church. Behind the offense called "the Church", however, looms a yet greater one, even though it is not often so clearly seen: Jesus Christ himself is the "stumbling block" that many people, even his disciples, run into. This offense is what today's Gospel is talking about.

First of all, his own family takes offense. Jesus is besieged by people. Everyone wants to see him, to touch him, to be healed by him. He cannot even find time to eat any more. His relations come to be persuaded that he is now really out of his senses, he is "nuts". When someone does not even take time to eat any more, there is something wrong with him.

How often, a new start being made by young people who want to devote their lives to some good cause, for their neighbor, or for God is wrecked by their own family: "Don't be crazy! Look after yourself, your career, earning a living!" Many calls from God have been stifled like that, and many vocations wrecked.

Jesus does not let his own family hold him back. There are greater things than one's own family. God's call takes priority. The family becomes a tyranny when it does not open itself for the will of God and free the one he is calling for his vocation.

That is why Jesus pronounces this saying about his mother and his relations—which only appears to be hard. It is not because she is his physical mother that she has a special place;

rather, it is because she, like no other, has done what God wills.

The family of Jesus is comprised of those people who do God's will. The ties of blood are strong, and they can become a prison unless God is set above all family relationships. There is something marvelous, on the other hand, about a physical family that also sticks together in faith. Only then do the ties of relationship fall into their proper place. And then many of the wounds that are so often in families can be healed.

The family after Jesus' own heart is the one where God's will is at the center, where Jesus brings about reconciliation and vouchsafes his healing presence. Such a family becomes a "house church", and when we look at it, it becomes clear what Jesus wants his Church to be like. It should be his family.

Worse than the reproach that Jesus is "out of his mind" is the accusation that he is possessed by the devil. That really deeply hurts Jesus. It is a total rejection of Jesus. Anyone who consciously and definitely maintains this view cannot be reached by Jesus' mercy. He is closing his heart against the Holy Spirit. Even God cannot and does not want to break down the doors to the heart of a man against his will if that man has locked them from within.

And Jesus talks quite coolly about the "kingdom of Satan". This is a reality; it is powerful and worldwide, with a strategy and a will directed to the destruction of good wherever possible. Yet Jesus also says something of great consolation: He is the stronger one who is breaking into the kingdom and the house of the Evil One and binding him in fetters. He alone can do this. That is why the kingdom of the Evil One fights against him, Christ the Lord, above all, and against the Church he supports and brings with him.

The Gospel of Mark 4:26-34

And [Jesus] said, "The kingdom of God is as if a man should scatter seed upon the ground, and should sleep and rise night and day, and the seed should sprout and grow, he knows not how. The earth produces of itself, first the blade, then the ear, then the full grain in the ear. But when the grain is ripe, at once he puts in the sickle, because the harvest has come."

And he said, "With what can we compare the kingdom of God, or what parable shall we use for it? It is like a grain of mustard seed, which, when sown upon the ground, is the smallest of all the seeds on earth; yet when it is sown it grows up and becomes the greatest of all shrubs, and puts forth large branches, so that the birds of the air can make nests in its shade."

With many such parables he spoke the word to them, as they were able to hear it; he did not speak to them without a parable, but privately to his own disciples he explained everything.

And Yet It Grows

How does God's kingdom grow? Can you see it, measure it, reckon it up, or predict it? How often Jesus talks about God's kingdom and about its growth! He talks about it mostly in parables.

He uses pictures from the everyday life of those times, experiences everyone might have. And yet he always breaks apart the obvious picture. He shows that daily life is not mundane. Everything can become something at which to marvel. For nothing is obvious to someone who has not forgotten how to marvel at things.

What is more normal than seed being sown? And then the seed lies in the ground. And look: it is growing. Day and night, whether the sower is thinking about it or not, the seed grows and grows. "Automatically" is what the Greek text says. "Of itself" is how our English Bible translates it; the earth brings forth fruit literally "of its own volition", "first the blade, then the ear, then the full grain in the ear", and Jesus adds that the man "knows not how".

No one knows. Scientists have learned a great deal. Our knowledge has grown tremendously. Nowadays we are able to know incomparably more than our forefathers did. What always amazes me is the strange fact that our contemporaries are not more struck with wonder than our forefathers. For more knowledge leads, not to greater conceit, but to a greater wonder. At least, that is how it should be.

The more we know about nature, about life and the way it "functions", the more we ought to marvel at the One who created it all in such an inconceivably marvelous way, who ordered it, put it all together, and coordinated each thing with everything else. The more we know, the more improbable it becomes that all that represents nothing but the product of a mere game of chance.

But today's two parables about seeds and the way they grow are not concerned with natural science. Our wonder at the marvels of nature is meant to lead us to even greater wonder at the marvels of the supernatural realm.

The kingdom of God is growing, "you know not how".

We human beings contribute to this as the sower does when he sows the seed. Yet he has neither made the seed himself, nor does he produce the "automatic" growth. "Nature", and the One who made nature, takes care of that.

So it is with the kingdom of God. Parents can sow the seed of faith in their children's hearts. They can encourage its growth, but they cannot "manufacture" their children's faith.

God remains the one who gives grace and faith. He sends growth as his gift to let the fruit of his action ripen.

How do things look as far as concerns the growth of the kingdom of God? Do we not have, rather, a lack of growth or even a negative growth in matters of faith? I fear that a great deal suggests a decline of this kind.

And yet, God remains the sovereign Lord of growth and harvest. One example that greatly moved me: in Wadowice, a little Polish town near Krakow. In 1920, in the parish church there, a child was baptized with the name of Karol. A seed was sown, as small as a mustard seed. This Karol died on April 2, 2005, as Pope John Paul II. A giant tree grew up from a tiny mustard seed of faith. Many were able to nest in its branches. He, above all others, freed the world from Communism and gave courage and hope to many people. And the kingdom of God has grown.

The Gospel of Mark 4:35-41

On that day, when evening had come, [Jesus] said to them, "Let us go across to the other side." And leaving the crowd, they took him with them, just as he was, in the boat. And other boats were with him. And a great storm of wind arose, and the waves beat into the boat, so that the boat was already filling. But he was in the stern, asleep on the cushion; and they woke him and said to him, "Teacher, do you not care if we perish?" And he awoke and rebuked the wind, and said to the sea, "Peace! Be still!" And the wind ceased, and there was a great calm. He said to them, "Why are you afraid? Have you no faith?" And they were filled with awe, and said to one another, "Who then is this, that even wind and sea obey him?"

Faith in the Storm

"Do you not care if we perish?" The disciples' cry for help in danger during the storm on the lake is something we know all about. The ship is in danger of sinking—and Jesus is sleeping as if nothing is happening. Even these fishermen from the Lake of Gennesaret, skilled and experienced sailors, are seized with panic and fear—and Jesus seems to be unaware and unconcerned.

This situation is repeated in every possible shape and form. God often seems not to be there in the midst of life's storms.

Whenever trouble and distress bring us to the verge of ruin, it is as if Christ were sleeping, as if he could neither hear nor see what is happening to us. Today's Gospel is speaking to that situation; it makes us feel both ashamed and, at the same time, consoled.

The Lake of Gennesaret is well known for its sudden and violent storms. This would not have been the first boat to sink in one of them. A few years ago, a fishing boat like this from the time of Jesus was discovered. It is now the pride of the museum at Kinereth Kibbutz. The disciples know well enough what danger they are in.

The fact that they lose their heads and panic completely must certainly make them ashamed afterward. For after all, their Master has talked so much about trust in God and about the fact that they can always be sure they are held safe in his hand. In their fright at the way the waves rose on the lake, it is as if all these lovely pious notions have been blown away. All that is left is their bare anxiety to survive.

And how many situations of the storm-on-the-lake type there are in life! Whenever all that remains in a relationship is conflict; whenever our own economic position brings us close to disaster; whenever the ground is moving and shaking in our spiritual life: Where is God at times like that? Is he asleep? Has he forgotten me? How does my faith help me now? Maybe God is asleep? Have I let him go to sleep; when everything was going nicely, did I forget "the good Lord", did I neglect my faith? Is it surprising if, now that there is a sudden emergency, he is not awake to help me through the storm? Like any attitude in life, faith has to be practiced in good times in order to be lively in bad. If I do not make it my habit to thank God when I am fortunate, then in an emergency I shall not have the confidence in God that can carry me through.

The scene in the Gospel is consoling: even the apostles lose hold of their faith and trust in an hour of great distress— at least to start with. Jesus brings them back out of their confusion, however. He makes the storm still. He restores their faith. And they ask themselves, shamefacedly, "When have we not trusted?" The next time, they will remember this. There will certainly be difficulties and distressing situations in the future, too. God does not spare us these. Yet they know this: Jesus is in the boat with me in life. Even when all seems lost, he will stand up and help me. I am never lost, with him. He is my Savior.

———

The Gospel of Mark 5:21–43

And when Jesus had crossed again in the boat to the other side, a great crowd gathered about him; and he was beside the sea. Then came one of the rulers of the synagogue, Jairus by name; and seeing him, he fell at his feet, and begged him, saying, "My little daughter is at the point of death. Come and lay your hands on her, so that she may be made well, and live." And he went with him.

And a great crowd followed him and thronged about him. And there was a woman who had had a flow of blood for twelve years, and who had suffered much under many physicians, and had spent all that she had, and was no better but rather grew worse. She had heard the reports about Jesus, and came up behind him in the crowd and touched his garment. For she said, "If I touch even his garments, I shall be made well." And immediately the hemorrhage ceased; and she felt in her body that she was healed of her disease. And Jesus, perceiving in himself that power had gone forth from him, immediately turned about in the crowd, and said, "Who touched my garments?" And his disciples said to him, "You see the crowd pressing around you, and yet you say, 'Who touched me?'" And he looked around to see who had done it. But the woman, knowing what had been done to her, came in fear and trembling and fell down before him, and told him the whole truth. And he said to her, "Daughter, your faith has made you well; go in peace, and be healed of your disease."

While he was still speaking, there came from the ruler's house some who said, "Your daughter is dead. Why trouble the Teacher any further?" But ignoring what they said, Jesus said to the ruler of the synagogue, "Do not fear, only believe." And he allowed no one to follow him except Peter and James and John the brother of James. When they came to the house of the ruler of the synagogue, he saw a tumult, and people weeping and wailing loudly. And when he had entered, he said to them, "Why do you make a tumult and weep? The child is not dead but sleeping." And they laughed at him. But he put them all outside, and took the child's father and mother and those who were with him, and went in where the child was. Taking her by the hand he said to her, "Talitha cumi"; which means, "Little girl, I say to you, arise." And immediately the girl got up and walked; for she was twelve years old. And immediately they were overcome with amazement. And he strictly charged them that no one should know this, and told them to give her something to eat.

ह

Only One Death Should Be Feared

How vividly these two of Jesus' miracles are recounted! A few words are enough for the evangelist Mark to make the two scenes come alive so we can almost see and touch them. Everywhere, people are telling others about Jesus. People throng together, they want to see Jesus, hear him, and touch him. His healings of the sick arouse many people's hopes. People in distress surge toward him from every direction. And since suffering has no favorites but picks on old and young, rich and poor alike, we find all kinds of people among those seeking his help. Trouble really does teach you to ask and pray for things!

How moving the synagogue ruler's request is: "My little daughter is at the point of death!" His beloved child must not die! No one can help—except Jesus, and in his trouble he trusts him completely.

Among those who trust Jesus and who are hoping for his help is a woman who is there in the crowd pressing close about Jesus. "A flow of blood"—that makes her ritually unclean. She is excluded from all religious life and is not allowed to touch anyone, so as not to make anyone else unclean. She has sought in vain for help from doctors, but that only cost money and brought no healing. She hopes that, in all the crowd, she may be able to touch Jesus without being noticed. Her touch does not go unnoticed, either on his side or on hers. Both of them feel that a power has been at work, coming out of him and healing her. Jesus is looking for her, not to expose her, but to praise her faith.

Faith is what he demands from Jairus, too, when Jairus is told that his child is dead: "Do not fear, only believe." The way that Jesus "wakes" the girl from death with just one word is something that will never be forgotten by the three apostles he takes with him into the room of death. They remembered it in Jesus' mother tongue: "Talitha cumi!"

Jesus wrought these two miracles for quite specific people in their particular situation of need. The story of them was written down for us, though. Why? So that we should get to know Jesus better. He takes us with him on his way and lets us see how he goes to work and who he is. He is the "Savior", healing wrongs. Wherever he comes, healing and wholeness take place. He heals bodily illness, and not only in those days. Up to this day, miracles of that kind are happening in his name and through his power. The accounts of them fill whole libraries; more still have never been written down yet take place in quite concrete and genuine fashion.

And up to this day, Jesus lets himself be touched by us. In all the sacraments, and especially in the Eucharist, we touch, not merely "the hem of his garment", but his very self. And from all the sacraments, a "power goes forth from him", a power that can heal the body and can pervade the soul. Thus, the woman who suffered from a flow of blood is, for all time, the example of faith that has the confidence to touch Jesus and is touched by Jesus.

"The child is only sleeping", says Jesus, to the mockery of those who are keening and mourning around the child. Jesus knows that she is dead, but not for eternity. Even if he has awakened the child from death (and that was going to happen many more times, in the history of the Church), she will still die again some day, or, as we say, "pass away". Jesus is Lord even of death.

That is why we do not need to be afraid of the "sleep" of death. The only thing we have to be afraid of is the "second death", something from which we pray the Lord will keep us all safe: the death of eternal separation from God. That is why there is nothing more urgent than to trust in Jesus wholly and completely—and to believe in him!

————

The Gospel of Mark 6:1b–6

[Jesus] came to his own country; and his disciples followed him. And on the sabbath he began to teach in the synagogue; and many who heard him were astonished, saying, "Where did this man get all this? What is the wisdom given to him? What mighty works are wrought by his hands! Is not this the carpenter, the son of Mary and brother of James and Joses and Judas and Simon, and are not his sisters here with us?" And they took offense at him. And Jesus said to them, "A prophet is not without honor, except in his own country, and among his own kin, and in his own house." And he could do no mighty work there, except that he laid his hands upon a few sick people and healed them. And he marveled because of their unbelief.

And he went about among the villages teaching.

❧

Do We Know One Another?

A disappointment at home. Jesus had lived in Nazareth for nearly thirty years, in the village in Galilee that at that time was neither famous nor important. That was where he grew up; where, presumably, he went to the synagogue school, learned his father's trade and practiced it. That was where his relations lived, his "brothers and sisters", as they are called in accordance with Jewish custom.

Jesus was about thirty years old when he suddenly set out down to the Lake of Gennesaret, to Capernaum, which lay on the great commercial route from the East to the Mediterranean. He soon became famous. His words held people spellbound, and his miracles perhaps even more so, the many healings of every kind of disease.

And now, for the first time, he had come back home again to Nazareth. Naturally, the news had spread that everyone was talking about the carpenter, Mary's son. Everywhere, people were talking about him. Curiosity was the first reaction of the people in his village when on the Saturday, the sabbath, he began to make a public speech in front of them, too. They were amazed at him; but the mood quickly changed. Criticisms were expressed: "After all, we know who he is. We've known him since he was only little. Who does he think he is? He's just one of us, no better than the rest of us! How come he thinks he can preach to us, the people from his hometown?"

Jesus was surprised and wounded by this rejection. Who does not want recognition, especially back home? Instead, he found jealousy and incomprehension. Jesus said something then that has remained a proverb up to this day: A prophet is without honor in his own country! How often that has proved painfully true. Someone's own people think that they know him particularly well—and they often know so little about him. The family can be tyrannical: no one is allowed to break out, to be different, to go his own way. To start with, it was like that with Jesus' relations. First of all, they thought he was crazy and wanted to bring him back by force, as Mark tells us. Later, things changed. James, one of the four "brothers of Jesus" mentioned here, even became head of the young Church in Jerusalem. It was only gradually that they realized who Jesus really was, this Jesus whom they thought they had known ever since childhood, because he had grown up with them and was, after all, one of them himself.

I think this disappointing experience at Nazareth shows us two things in particular. The first is true only of Jesus: How were his neighbors in the village and his relations to know that the child who grew up in their midst bore within him such a secret, that he was God's Son made man? His everyday life in Nazareth was too unassuming. It is a little bit like that right up to the present day. God's presence in our midst is often hidden and easy to overlook. Today, too, Christ is with us in "everyday clothes", and only the eyes of faith perceive him.

The second applies to us all: How easily we are mistaken about those people closest to us! Everyone has his secret, his unsuspected qualities. It is often those outside, strangers, who are more aware of these than the person's own family, who think they already know all about him. How lovely it is when we rediscover what treasures are to be found in other people!

The Gospel of Mark 6:7-13

And [Jesus] called to him the Twelve, and began to send them out two by two, and gave them authority over the unclean spirits. He charged them to take nothing for their journey except a staff; no bread, no bag, no money in their belts; but to wear sandals and not put on two tunics. And he said to them, "Where you enter a house, stay there until you leave the place. And if any place will not receive you and they refuse to hear you, when you leave, shake off the dust that is on your feet for a testimony against them." So they went out and preached that men should repent. And they cast out many demons, and anointed with oil many that were sick and healed them.

On Holy Fools

You rub your eyes and ask yourself, "Did I really see that?" That is how it was at the beginning of the Church: Jesus sent his first disciples out without any food satchel, with no money, wearing sandals and carrying a pilgrim's staff, to bring the gospel to men. And what came of this? Has the Church long since betrayed this ideal? How do the successors of the apostles live today? And can they, do they, do what Jesus instructed the first apostles to do: drive out demons and heal the sick? Do the current successors of the apostles believe in the devil and in demons at all? And in their task of setting people free from their clutches? Do the current disciples of Jesus believe that their Master has given them the task and the authority, not merely to comfort sick people, but to heal them?

The gospel is a dangerous looking glass. Anyone who looks into it has to be ready to have his life called into question. What do I see there, as a bishop and successor of the apostles? What do parish priests see in this looking glass, in our present situation? What do you see, dear reader, in these words of Jesus, which are, after all, addressed to all men?

There is one easy way around this self-critical questioning: saying that that was the gospel for that age, for the heroic times at the beginning. There was a need then for such radical people, who went out poor and powerless and without financial means, armed only with the power of Jesus and of his Spirit, to proclaim the gospel. Since then, the Church has spread all over the world, has set up her structures—congregations, parishes, and so on—and despite many weaknesses, she has been working surprisingly well for nearly two thousand years now.

This is too easy a way of dealing with it. Francis of Assisi (1181–1226) was not satisfied with this explanation, and no more was Mother Teresa of Calcutta (1910–1997). Time and again, there have been these "holy fools" who took the gospel literally. The founder of my own order, Saint Dominic (1170–1221), was one of those (I belong to the Dominican order). He really did leave all wealth behind to set off on foot, poor and trusting entirely in God, to preach the good news. And the amazing thing, once again, is that these "fools" who followed Jesus have renewed the Church, have aroused her from her slumber of security. They have brought the fresh air of the gospel into the stuffy atmosphere of an all-too-well-organized Church. And that is possible even in the gorgeous palace of the Vatican—just think of good Pope John XXIII (1881–1962).

What does that mean for a present-day bishop or a parish priest or any one of us? Even if we do not set out with sandals and a pilgrim's staff nowadays—though some people do this even today—yet I can nonetheless free myself, inwardly, can remain mobile, a pilgrim on this earthly way, ready to leave behind all the baggage that collects and to trust in the power of Jesus, which heals us and sets us free from the snares of the Evil One. Thus anyone, even at home, can be an apostle.

The Gospel of Mark 6:30-34

The apostles returned to Jesus, and told him all that they had done and taught. And he said to them, "Come away by yourselves to a lonely place, and rest awhile." For many were coming and going, and they had no leisure even to eat. And they went away in the boat to a lonely place by themselves. Now many saw them going, and knew them, and they ran there on foot from all the towns, and got there ahead of them. As he landed he saw a great throng, and he had compassion on them, because they were like sheep without a shepherd; and he began to teach them many things.

ॐ

A Different Kind of Holiday

Today's Gospel is suitable for holidays and vacations: "Rest awhile!" There is a time for working and a time for resting from our work. Jesus lets his colleagues, the apostles, have some time for rest and refreshment, after they have completed a period of strenuous employment: "Come away with me to a lonely place, where we can be on our own, and rest awhile."

Holidays of the kind Jesus is planning with his friends ought not to be a further hectic period of stress, full of experiences and changes and dissipation. That is not really taking a rest, coming to rest, to a standstill. Jesus wants to have time with the disciples, in peace and away from all the bustle, simply to be together. They should be able to "refuel" in company with him and among themselves. Noisy places, where there is always bustle and noise, are unsuitable for that. Jesus himself often goes off to look for solitude, preferably in the mountains, away from all human activity. He finds his "relaxation" in silence and prayer. Many people today are, quite rightly, seeking with renewed emphasis such forms of "holidays for the soul".

On that occasion, of course, things turn out quite differently. It is not the tranquility of a lonely place that is awaiting the apostles, in their real need for relaxation, but an enormous crowd who want to see Jesus, to touch him, and to hear him.

I myself had a similar experience in Africa, two years ago, when we crossed a lake in a boat to a village where I was to hold a service. We saw hordes of people running along the shore. They got there before us, and when we disembarked a vast crowd was waiting for us.

I am trying to imagine the faces the apostles make when they see all those people: absolutely no peace and quiet, yet again! No kind of rest, again, no relaxation! But the evangelist Mark says nothing about that. All that interests him is Jesus' attitude: not a word of impatience or of irritation that the plans for a time of relaxation have come to nothing. He gives his entire attention to the people who have come running to him, full of expectation, with their worries, their trouble, and their illnesses—many of them are indeed suffering, exhausted, their faces marked by life's trials. He does not think about his well-earned rest, his "holiday"; rather, he thinks about all the people who are now looking to him with hope. And he looks upon them with great sympathy and sees their difficulties and the hard life they have, what burdens they have to bear.

And now comes the amazing thing: Jesus reacts to the people's need, which goes to his heart, in an unusual way: "He taught them many things", until it was evening, and the disciples' stomachs are rumbling, reminding them that it is time to eat, even if they have not found the rest to which they have been looking forward.

Jesus takes pity, above all, on the aimlessness of the people who come running after him. More than everything, he wants to show them first of all the way that leads to life and happiness. He gives them his gospel first of all and, then, also bread for their bodies (see next Sunday). We, thank God, have bread enough for us. But we urgently need direction. That is what Jesus is giving in his gospel, even today, freely and plentifully. We simply have to take time for this, a meaningful holiday.

The Gospel of John 6:1–15

After this Jesus went to the other side of the Sea of Galilee, which is the Sea of Tiberias. And a multitude followed him, because they saw the signs which he did on those who were diseased. Jesus went up into the hills, and there sat down with his disciples. Now the Passover, the feast of the Jews, was at hand. Lifting up his eyes, then, and seeing that a multitude was coming to him, Jesus said to Philip, "How are we to buy bread, so that these people may eat?" This he said to test him, for he himself knew what he would do. Philip answered him, "Two hundred denarii would not buy enough bread for each of them to get a little." One of his disciples, Andrew, Simon Peter's brother, said to him, "There is a lad here who has five barley loaves and two fish; but what are they among so many?" Jesus said, "Make the people sit down." Now there was much grass in the place; so the men sat down, in number about five thousand. Jesus then took the loaves, and when he had given thanks, he distributed them to those who were seated; so also the fish, as much as they wanted. And when they had eaten their fill, he told his disciples, "Gather up the fragments left over, that nothing may be lost." So they gathered them up and filled twelve baskets with fragments from the five barley loaves, left by those who had eaten. When the people saw the sign which he had done, they said, "This is indeed the prophet who is to come into the world!"

Perceiving then that they were about to come and take

him by force to make him king, Jesus withdrew again to the hills by himself.

ૢۻ

Where Shall We Find the Power?

When four people give reports about the same event, they will not all say exactly the same thing, for each of them will highlight certain details and will leave out many things that seem important to the others. And yet it is clear that this is one and the same event. The differences in the four reports, themselves, make the four witnesses still more trustworthy when it emerges that they are essentially in agreement. All four evangelists are talking about an especially impressive event in Jesus' life. He once (even twice, according to Mark and Matthew) abundantly satisfied the hunger of a very large crowd, who had with them nothing (or not enough) to eat, with just a few loaves of bread, so that in the end there were still several baskets full of bread left over.

I myself see no serious reason for doubting the credibility of these four witnesses. I also believe that Christ had (and still has) the power to perform a sign like that, which is known as "the feeding of the five thousand". There are, besides, a good many other similar miracles in the history of the Church for which there is plenty of evidence. I am thinking, for instance, of the flour bin in the orphanage of the saintly Curé of Ars (1786–1859). This flour bin, for a long time, was simply never empty when they were running very short in the orphanage and the children had hardly anything to eat.

The question is, Why do all four evangelists tell this story? Certainly, because it was very striking and made a great impression on people. Why did Jesus perform the miracle? John says that Jesus "knew what he would do". What induced him to do it? What is the message, so to speak, of this extraordinary event?

The four evangelists agree in attesting that Jesus was moved in the first instance by the quite simple concern about how all these people were to get something to eat. That is explicit in Mark. There, Jesus says, "I have compassion on the crowd, because they have been with me now three days, and have nothing to eat; and if I send them away hungry to their homes, they will faint on the way; and some of them have come a long way" (Mk 8:2–3) Jesus did not look away when he saw people suffering. He did not always turn all troubles away from people, but he himself never turned away from those in trouble.

And his will was, and is, that it should be no different where his disciples were concerned. That is why he tested them. He challenged them to help, and when they said, "You are asking us to do the impossible", then he showed them, "If you trust in me, then you will achieve incredible things, far beyond your own powers." Since then, many people have discovered for themselves the miracle of the way that our powers are multiplied if with God's help we put them at the service of dealing with other people's troubles.

But the more profound thing that Jesus himself wanted to show us in the feeding of the five thousand is something we will hear about over the next four Sundays.

EIGHTEENTH SUNDAY IN ORDINARY TIME

The Gospel of John 6:24–35

So when the people saw that Jesus was not there, nor his disciples, they themselves got into the boats and went to Capernaum, seeking Jesus.

When they found him on the other side of the sea, they said to him, "Rabbi, when did you come here?" Jesus answered them, "Truly, truly, I say to you, you seek me, not because you saw signs, but because you ate your fill of the loaves. Do not labor for the food which perishes, but for the food which endures to eternal life, which the Son of man will give to you; for on him has God the Father set his seal." Then they said to him, "What must we do, to be doing the works of God?" Jesus answered them, "This is the work of God, that you believe in him whom he has sent." So they said to him, "Then what sign do you do, that we may see, and believe you? What work do you perform? Our fathers ate the manna in the wilderness; as it is written, 'He gave them bread from heaven to eat.'" Jesus then said to them, "Truly, truly, I say to you, it was not Moses who gave you the bread from heaven; my Father gives you the true bread from heaven. For the bread of God is that which comes down from heaven, and gives life to the world." They said to him, "Lord, give us this bread always."

Jesus said to them, "I am the bread of life; he who comes to me shall not hunger, and he who believes in me shall never thirst."

The Bread of Love

Throwing bread away—that is something I still cannot do, even today. Anyone who has learned in childhood that bread is precious and that you do not simply throw bread away will never bring himself to do that, even later in life.

It is still shocking to see what great quantities of bread, and food in general, are simply thrown away and destroyed in our present-day society. It is not a blessed activity.

After the feeding of the five thousand, when Jesus had marvelously multiplied just five loaves so as to satisfy the hunger of the whole crowd, he had the leftover bread collected. That came to twelve full baskets. The Gospel does not tell us what happened to it. But we can certainly assume that it was not thrown away. Bread was simply too precious for that.

Jesus is now talking about a still more precious bread, however. Back in Capernaum, where Jesus was staying at the time, people came looking for him. What drew them? His reputation as a miracle worker or something more profound? Not only bread for their bodily hunger, but nourishment for their spiritual hunger?

People do feel this other hunger, and Jesus often talked about it, for instance, when he said, "Man shall not live by bread alone, but by every word that proceeds from the mouth of God" (Mt 4:4; cf. Deut 8:3). Today, he challenges us to be concerned, not merely with perishable food, but with that food which endures to eternal life.

The people listening to him understood, perhaps dimly, that this enduring food, which strengthens not only the body but also the soul, had something to do with the will of God. Only a life in harmony with God can satisfy the deep hunger of the soul. And so they asked him, "What must we do, for our life to be congruent with God?" The answer is surprising: Only faith can satisfy the hunger of the soul; not just any faith, such as faith in the power of the stars or belief in a blind fate or in secret forces, but personal faith in Jesus Christ.

It is understandable that his audience did not grasp that to start with. The fact that faith in God can strengthen and console one's spirit is something many people have experienced in their own lives. But believing in Jesus, who is after all merely a man, they found difficult. So they demanded a sign, a proof that they should believe in Jesus. They wanted to know why they should trust in him. Quite rightly, they did not want simply to believe blindly. That would have been irresponsible.

Once again, Jesus' response is surprising: "I am the bread of life." What Jesus is actually saying here is, "Your life comes from me. Anyone who takes me into his life will discover that I can wholly and completely satisfy his spirit's hunger and thirst."

Jesus says of himself that he is the true bread that God gives to men. Many people can confirm that, because they have experienced it in their own lives. They can witness to what Jesus promised, "He who comes to me shall not hunger." They have found in Jesus what their heart most profoundly longs for: knowing that they are loved, not finding themselves judged, being accepted, and being able to trust. They have found in Jesus the most important thing in life: the bread of love.

The Gospel of John 6:41–51

At that time the Jews murmured at [Jesus], because he said, "I am the bread which came down from heaven." They said, "Is not this Jesus, the son of Joseph, whose father and mother we know? How does he now say, 'I have come down from heaven'?" Jesus answered them, "Do not murmur among yourselves. No one can come to me unless the Father who sent me draws him; and I will raise him up at the last day. It is written in the prophets, 'And they shall all be taught by God.' Every one who has heard and learned from the Father comes to me. Not that any one has seen the Father except him who is from God; he has seen the Father. Truly, truly, I say to you, he who believes has eternal life. I am the bread of life. Your fathers ate the manna in the wilderness, and they died. This is the bread which comes down from heaven, that a man may eat of it and not die. I am the living bread which came down from heaven; if any one eats of this bread, he will live for ever; and the bread which I shall give for the life of the world is my flesh."

Yes, That's Really How It Is!

We can understand the people's grumbling. In the little village of Capernaum, beside Lake Gennesaret, there was someone who said he had come down from heaven. Perhaps then, two thousand years ago, people believed in miracles more easily than they do now. They had in any case really just experienced a powerful miracle: in an isolated spot, Jesus had fed that enormous crowd with only five loaves and two fishes; and he had provided so much more than enough that the leftover bread filled twelve baskets. This miracle is so credibly attested by all four Gospels that I see no serious reason for doubting it. Jesus' contemporaries certainly had no doubts, for in their enthusiasm over this miracle they wanted to choose Jesus for their king straightaway and thus make him the leader of the longed-for liberation from Roman rule.

Jesus, however, had another end in view. His mission was not one of political liberation. What he intended to give was not merely bread for bodily hunger, however much he was concerned that the people who came to him should not go away hungry.

He knew of another kind of food, which came, not from the earth, but from "heaven", from God. That, too, we can understand: we need spiritual food, food for our souls, as well. Our daily bread is necessary, but it is not enough. When love is lacking, and a meaning in life and hope, then a man faces spiritual ruin.

That was not the reason why the people were protesting in Capernaum; rather, it was because Jesus said that he himself was this "bread from heaven". He was "the bread of life", he said. What Jesus was saying about himself, then, was that he is the food that man needs in order to avoid withering away spiritually. How can any man say about himself that he is to some extent "spiritually necessary"? Has that not led in the past down many a dreadful false trail? Many people can still remember what it was like when Adolf Hitler was asserting that he brought salvation and when he had himself greeted as such. We are quite rightly warned against gurus and leaders of sects who let themselves be honored as bringers of salvation.

"Jesus is just a man, after all", was how the people who heard him reacted. "We know him, we know who his parents are." This critical attitude was sensible. People did not want to be taken in by some sectarian, a self-appointed messenger of salvation, for there was no lack of such people at that time any more than today.

Jesus did not immediately condemn this skeptical reticence. What he said was, rather: "Coming to me, believing in me, is possible only if God is leading someone to me in his heart." Faith is a gift. Believing in Jesus is something that goes beyond our understanding. Yet it is not foolish and irrational. Anyone who has experienced it can bear witness to that.

On my holidays I met a married couple who had both experienced an inner conversion at a place of pilgrimage. Before, they had been what we call "interested onlookers", not unbelieving, but rather inclined to stand back. They experienced what Jesus is talking about in this Gospel reading: Jesus had become for them, in quite a new way, the "bread of life". His teaching, his example, and fellowship with him had given their lives new meaning and a joy unknown to them before. Today they can say, "Yes, that's really how it is!"

The Gospel of John 6:51–58

[At that time, Jesus said to the crowd,] "I am the living bread which came down from heaven; if any one eats of this bread, he will live for ever; and the bread which I shall give for the life of the world is my flesh."

The Jews then disputed among themselves, saying, "How can this man give us his flesh to eat?" So Jesus said to them, "Truly, truly, I say to you, unless you eat the flesh of the Son of man and drink his blood, you have no life in you; he who eats my flesh and drinks my blood has eternal life, and I will raise him up at the last day. For my flesh is food indeed, and my blood is drink indeed. He who eats my flesh and drinks my blood abides in me, and I in him. As the living Father sent me, and I live because of the Father, so he who eats me will live because of me. This is the bread which came down from heaven, not such as the fathers ate and died; he who eats this bread will live for ever."

ঌ

Unacceptable?

Shortly before this, Jesus had reprimanded his disciples when they wanted to send the people away so that they could go and buy themselves bread in the neighboring villages. "You don't need to send the people away; give them something to eat yourselves", he had challenged them. And when the apostles could not manage that, Jesus multiplied the loaves and satisfied everyone's hunger. No wonder people were most enthusiastic about Jesus.

What Jesus did in his sermon at Capernaum had exactly the opposite effect, however. Now he was driving people away himself; and the longer he went on talking, the worse it got.

First he talked about another kind of bread, which satisfies the hunger of the soul. Then he declared that he himself was that bread. He said that he had come from heaven, that he was the "bread from heaven", and that anyone who ate this bread would live forever.

That was difficult enough to accept: someone whose family and provenance were known had supposedly come from heaven? It got worse, as Jesus continued; his statements grew more intense, not weaker: the bread he gave, and that he himself is, was his own flesh.

Try to imagine what kind of effect such words must have had on his audience. No wonder they gave rise to disputes and contradiction! Yet instead of soothing people and explaining things so as to calm them down, Jesus' assertions became more pointed. It sounded like deliberate provocation, an intolerable affront, when he said with emphasis, "He who eats my flesh and drinks my blood abides in me, and I in him." So that no doubt might remain, he added, "Unless you do that, 'you have no life in you.'"

He was saying, then, that people have to eat his flesh and drink his blood in order to live, to attain eternal life. And, moreover, in saying this, Jesus used the words for real eating (chewing with one's teeth) and genuine drinking.

Jesus' speech had "ongoing results": more and more people turned away from him; they went away and they stayed away. Why did he do that? Why did he make excessive demands on people? Or is he concerned not to withhold from us this mystery, the most profound mystery of his life and the hardest to understand? Perhaps what he is trying to entrust to us is so precious that he will risk shocking us?

What is this mystery? The fact that Jesus is trying to share not only some teaching with us but a life, his life, himself. He intends for God's life, which is within him, to become our life too, quite genuinely, like the food we take into us. "Eat me and drink me! Live from me, as I live within you": Is that so incomprehensible?

And if it were, after all, true? If God wanted to be so close to us that he himself became our food? Just as a child in his mother's womb lives entirely from his mother, and receives from her all that he needs to live and to grow, so Jesus lives relying entirely on his "intimacy with God". And that is the way he wants us to live from him: "Whoever eats me will live through me." Is that so unacceptable?

The Gospel of John 6:60–69

Many of his disciples, when they heard [his teaching],
said, "This is a hard saying; who can listen to it?" But
Jesus, knowing in himself that his disciples murmured at it,
said to them, "Do you take offense at this? Then what if
you were to see the Son of man ascending where he was
before? It is the Spirit that gives life, the flesh is of no avail;
the words that I have spoken to you are Spirit and life. But
there are some of you that do not believe." For Jesus knew
from the first who those were that did not believe, and who
it was that would betray him. And he said, "This is why I
told you that no one can come to me unless it is granted him
by the Father."

After this many of his disciples drew back and no longer
walked with him. Jesus said to the Twelve, "Will you also
go away?" Simon Peter answered him, "Lord, to whom
shall we go? You have the words of eternal life; and we
have believed, and have come to know, that you are the
Holy One of God."

಄

Will You Go, Too?

Many went away at that time, not only from among the
"interested onlookers", but also from the innermost circle.
Many of his disciples said at that time, when they listened to
Jesus, "What he is saying is intolerable; who can listen to it?"

Many of his disciples stopped going around with him at that time.

Was it only then that things were that way? A strange turnaround. Just a few days earlier, thousands had come, drawn by the reputation that preceded Jesus: he heals sick people, sets free those who are possessed, works miracles, and perhaps he is even going to bring liberation from the yoke of the Roman occupation. As quickly as the hope flared up, it died down again. They went away disappointed. They regarded his words as unacceptable, even intolerable: they were supposed to eat his flesh, and to drink his blood? A lunatic thing to say! "Who can listen to it?"

Why this about-face? First of all, enthusiasm—they even wanted to make him king—and then total rejection; people turning away in fury, a fury that would go as far as "Crucify him!" How did this change of mood come about?

In my childhood, the churches were full to overflowing. Today, there are often no more than a handful of people who come to worship on a Sunday. Why this about-face? Whose fault is it?

Is it the fault of "the Church" that she is not (any longer) attractive? Is it the changed times, people's different way of life? Or is it Jesus himself? Are people no longer interested in his words and in what he has to offer? Have his words become alien, remote from our age? Even, perhaps, intolerable? Are many people turning away because they can no longer make anything of his teaching? Are there many who no longer join in because they take offense?

These are the questions that concern me when I read how Jesus got on in Capernaum that time. Is all that being repeated today, perhaps? One thing is sure: then, as now, Jesus fully respects our freedom. Time and again, in the Church, pressure and force have been used—but Jesus certainly never used them. "Will you also go away?" To this day, Jesus puts that question—and the answer can only come freely, from the heart.

Then, it was Peter who provided the answer. It is moving, on account of its honesty: "Lord, to whom shall we go?" That does not, perhaps, sound very complimentary, but it comes from the heart: We don't know where we should go, to whom we should turn: "You have the words of eternal life."

Is Peter not saying something there that goes to our hearts even today? "In fact, I do not understand a great deal of what you say, or not yet. What that means, that we should eat your flesh and drink your blood, I find hard to grasp. Nevertheless, I will not and cannot desert you. For we have never met anyone like you. No one has ever talked to us the way you do. Even if there is a great deal that I don't understand in what you say and do, there is one thing I really have grasped: that you are the Holy One of God."

You, and no one else! That was the experience that motivated Peter and a few others to stay with Jesus. They believed in him; they trusted him and loved him. To this day, that is the essential decision. Those who have decided to stay with him have never regretted it.

The Gospel of Mark 7:1–8, 14–15, 21–23

Now when the Pharisees gathered together to him, with some of the scribes, who had come from Jerusalem, they saw that some of his disciples ate with hands defiled, that is, unwashed. (For the Pharisees, and all the Jews, do not eat unless they wash their hands, observing the tradition of the elders; and when they come from the market place, they do not eat unless they purify themselves; and there are many other traditions which they observe, the washing of cups and pots and vessels of bronze.) And the Pharisees and the scribes asked him, "Why do your disciples not live according to the tradition of the elders, but eat with hands defiled?" And he said to them, "Well did Isaiah prophesy of you hypocrites, as it is written,

'This people honors me with their lips,

but their heart is far from me;

in vain do they worship me,

teaching as doctrines the precepts of men.'

You leave the commandment of God, and hold fast the tradition of men.". . .

And he called the people to him again, and said to them, "Hear me, all of you, and understand: there is nothing outside a man which by going into him can defile him; but the things which come out of a man are what defile him. . . .

"For from within, out of the heart of man, come evil thoughts, fornication, theft, murder, adultery, coveting, wickedness, deceit, licentiousness, envy, slander, pride,

foolishness. All these evil things come from within, and they defile a man."

៚

What Comes Out of the Heart

"Wash your hands before eating!" How often I heard that as a child. If I had known this Gospel reading then, a cheeky answer to my parents would have burst out of me, "But after all, Jesus' disciples didn't wash their hands before eating."

Why did they not do it? From sloppiness, from laziness? As a protest against prescribed customs? It was for these reasons that, as children or as young people, we left off washing our hands in the usual way, knowing that our parents would correct us for it.

Was Jesus a protester? Did he encourage his disciples to rebel against the rules of correct behavior obtaining in his day? It might seem like that at first sight. What is there to make a fuss about in washing your hands when you come in from the dirty, dusty market? It makes sense, after all, to clean yourself up before starting your meal. And washing the crockery you use for cooking and eating is a sensible rule of hygiene.

But this dispute was about more than rules for good health. All this cleansing had also a religious side to it. Dirty hands make a man unclean: that was what the old prescriptions of the Jewish law said.

Anyone who did not practice these acts of cleansing was not ready for prayer or for worship, so the elders taught.

That is what Jesus was protesting against; not against washing one's hands or washing the crockery. The person who is unclean before God is not the one with dirty hands but the one whose heart is full of hate.

"Hear me, all of you, and understand." Jesus is concerned with something important that he wants to say to everyone: All external activity is empty and hypocritical unless it comes from the heart. It is not the person who behaves in a pious fashion who is pleasing to God; it is the one who is good from his heart. What use are all possible external practices if they are hollow within?

"Hypocrisy" is what Jesus calls such behavior. There was nothing he attacked so strongly. For it is not appearance that counts before God, but reality; not the way someone presents himself, but what he really is. Jesus always loved and praised what was genuine.

What should we understand from this? That evil comes from within, from our hearts. That is where evil thoughts come from, and they then lead to wicked acts. Jesus mentions no less than thirteen evil things that all come out of a wicked heart. We must cleanse our hearts, for their filth is much worse than that on dirty hands or dirty pots.

Two basic thoughts on this: It is true that all evil comes from the heart. Yet it may also have been let into the heart beforehand. How much evil comes into our hearts from malicious slander and nasty gossip—if we accept it. How many evil pictures can take root in our minds through videos, the internet, and television. They can gradually poison our heart: that is a new danger for our hearts today.

So, from the heart comes all evil. Yet everything good, as well: loving thoughts and actions, those of kindness and understanding, and above all mercy, which no one gives us so generously as Jesus. For there is nothing false or feigned in his heart. That is the important thing, not washing one's hands.

The Gospel of Mark 7:31–37

Then [Jesus] returned from the region of Tyre, and went through Sidon to the Sea of Galilee, through the region of the Decapolis. And they brought to him a man who was deaf and had an impediment in his speech; and they begged him to lay his hand upon him. And taking him aside from the multitude privately, he put his fingers into his ears, and he spat and touched his tongue; and looking up to heaven, he sighed, and said to him, "Ephphatha," that is, "Be opened." And his ears were opened, his tongue was released, and he spoke plainly. And he charged them to tell no one; but the more he charged them, the more zealously they proclaimed it. And they were astonished beyond measure, saying, "He has done all things well; he even makes the deaf hear and the mute speak."

❧

Be Opened!

Not to be able to hear and not to be able to speak—anyone with both these gifts can hardly imagine what that means. Not being able to hear any music or the roar of the surf or any bird song or anything of all the everyday noises that sometimes weary us but that are yet a part of life—that must be hard to bear. And when being mute is added to the deafness—not hearing a word and also being unable to speak a single word—then the suffering must be much worse still.

Only if we think about it, when we meet people who are deaf and mute, do we realize what a precious thing it is to be able to use our ears and our mouth, our hearing and our speech. Perhaps we become aware of how often they are misused, maybe when we lend an ear to all kinds of gossip and mischievous idle talk or even spread it abroad with our own mouths.

Marvelous things are possible today to improve the communications of deaf and mute people with their fellowmen, and marvelous things are accomplished by the deaf and mute themselves. Just recently, at the airport, I saw a whole group of deaf and mute people who were holding an animated conversation by means of their sign language.

In Jesus' day, the lot of deaf and mute people was still more onerous. One of them was brought to Jesus. People took pity on him and thought that Jesus might be able to do the impossible and help him—even heal him.

These people must have had enormous trust in Jesus. They were probably pagans, not Jews, since the area of the Decapolis was (and still is today) outside Israel. Their deep and genuine sympathy for the disabled person moved them to take this step, turning in trust to Jesus.

Jesus was prepared to help. But not in front of the inquisitive crowd. This was not to be a public spectacle. So he carefully took him to one side, just the two of them. His actions were simple and comprehensible. He touched the disabled part, showing how moved he was by the suffering of the disabled person. His sigh was a wordless plea to heaven, to God, his Father. With his divine power, he pronounced the liberating word that resolved the problem: "Be opened!" The man's ears were opened, his tongue threw off its bonds, and the man could hear and speak properly.

What happened then for a deaf and mute man, amazing as

it is, is a sign for us all. Worse than being physically deaf is having a deaf heart, when we can no longer hear someone else's voice for the sheer noise and racket of everyday life or perhaps that of our own selfishness; when we become deaf to what God is trying to say to us through his Word or through other people.

Worse than being bodily mute is having love fall silent between us, when people maintain a cold silence toward another or when bitterness, disappointments, and hurts close people's mouths so that no kindly word comes forth any more.

Whenever we notice that happening, when it happens to us, then we should bring one another to Jesus, so that he may touch us. Then the still greater miracle can happen of his opening our ears and our mouth anew, so that we listen to one another once more and begin to talk to one another; so that God may speak anew to our hearts and may open up our deaf and mute hearts. "He has done all things well", we will then be able to say, in gratitude and wonder.

The Gospel of Mark 8:27–35

And Jesus went on with his disciples, to the villages of Caesarea Philippi; and on the way he asked his disciples, "Who do men say that I am?" And they told him, "John the Baptist; and others say, Elijah; and others one of the prophets." And he asked them, "But who do you say that I am?" Peter answered him, "You are the Christ." And he charged them to tell no one about him.

And he began to teach them that the Son of man must suffer many things, and be rejected by the elders and the chief priests and the scribes, and be killed, and after three days rise again. And he said this plainly. And Peter took him, and began to rebuke him. But turning and seeing his disciples, he rebuked Peter, and said, "Get behind me, Satan! For you are not on the side of God, but of men."

And he called to him the multitude with his disciples, and said to them, "If any man would come after me, let him deny himself and take up his cross and follow me. For whoever would save his life will lose it; and whoever loses his life for my sake and the gospel's will save it."

The Crucified Messiah

Saint Mark has one basic aim in his Gospel: bringing his hearers and his readers to recognize Jesus as being the one he describes in the first sentence of his Gospel, "Jesus the Christ (Messiah), the Son of God", and to confess him as such.

And indeed, there are two parts to his Gospel. At the end of the first, in today's Gospel reading, Peter confesses that Jesus is the Messiah, the Anointed, the Christ. At the end of the second part, there is the confession of the (pagan) Roman centurion, "Truly this man was the Son of God!" (Mk 15:39).

The path leading up to this dual confession, two recognitions that are closely connected, leads through many a trial and receives its final attestation beneath the Cross.

The Jews were hoping (and still are hoping) for the coming of the Messiah. Then everything (they hope) will be put right. He will finally bring liberation. Peace will reign in his time; all will fare well on earth, not just in the distant heaven.

For Jesus' disciples, this question, whether explicit or implicit, must have been at the heart of their hopes and expectations from the beginning. Naturally they wondered (at least in their hearts) whether Jesus was the promised Messiah or not. And they hoped that he was.

Thus, Jesus' question, "Who do men say that I am?" was not wholly unexpected. The apostles, who had their ear to the ground along with ordinary people, were able to answer straight off, "A prophet!" That is the way it has been, to this day. Many people see in Jesus no more (and no less) than a prophet. For many people these days, their awareness of his inmost mystery seems to be fading. Many people find it hard to believe that he is God's Son and that all the hopes of mankind are fulfilled in him. It is a lot easier to regard him as one of the great prophets in the history of mankind, along with Buddha, Moses, and Muhammad.

"But who do you say that I am?" It is a completely direct and personal question. Not, what do "people" say, what does "everybody" think, but you, personally. To this day, the question is suddenly there in our lives: "Who am I, Jesus, for you? Are you giving me your real, personal answer?"

Peter gives the answer without hesitation, concisely: "You are the Messiah, the Christ." That is not merely a neutral observation. I should almost want to say that it is a declaration of love. It is a confession of faith that turns into an expression of personal loyalty, an expression of hope: "You are the one we have longed for; you have been our hope for generations already."

Peter has scarcely uttered this—surely on behalf of the other apostles, too—when Jesus "applies the brakes": "Don't talk to anyone else about this!" Why is there this ban on shouting out loud such joyful news? Because so many misunderstandings are looming. Because such misconceived hopes will be placed on the Messiah. Because his coming is associated, above all, with political expectations.

How much Peter in particular still has to learn about understanding in what sense Jesus is "the Messiah" is immediately apparent when Jesus starts to talk "quite openly" about the suffering that lies before him. The Messiah has to suffer, instead of liberating people? Peter simply cannot allow this. Never again will he have to suffer such a sharp rebuff: "Behind me, Satan!" (That is a literal translation.) "Only if you follow me along the path to the Cross will you understand the way in which the Messiah effects his task of liberating people: not by armed force, but by the powerlessness of love." Not even death can touch love, for "after three days he will rise again". Then you can, and must, tell everyone, "Jesus is the Messiah, the Son of God!"

The Gospel of Mark 9:30–37

[Jesus and his disciples] went on from there and passed through Galilee. And he would not have any one know it; for he was teaching his disciples, saying to them, "The Son of man will be delivered into the hands of men, and they will kill him; and when he is killed, after three days he will rise." But they did not understand the saying, and they were afraid to ask him.

And they came to Capernaum; and when he was in the house he asked them, "What were you discussing on the way?" But they were silent; for on the way they had discussed with one another who was the greatest. And he sat down and called the Twelve and he said to them, "If any one would be first, he must be last of all and servant of all." And he took a child, and put him in the midst of them; and taking him in his arms, he said to them, "Whoever receives one such child in my name receives me; and whoever receives me, receives not me but him who sent me."

A Child in the Midst

Amazing, how honest the apostles were! "What were you discussing on the way?"

They fell silent at this question from Jesus. Understandably, since they were ashamed to admit what had been the subject of their discussions on the way. They had been doing what constantly happens, to this day, even in the Church and among Christians: "They had discussed with one another who was the greatest."

Who is the greatest, the best, the most successful? How often it is all about that! And how often we try to climb to the top ourselves, shoving our way up and necessarily shoving other people down. How often we try to show ourselves in a good light, whether consciously or not, and to cast others into shadow . . .

The honesty with which the apostles admitted that they had, unfortunately, been no exception in this respect is amazing.

For me, that is one of the strongest arguments in favor of the credibility and reliability of the Gospels.

They do not offer us a sugarcoated story. They show men of flesh and blood. Yet they do not stop at that; rather, they show us how we can find our way out of the old self-centeredness, how to overcome the old attitude of "I'm the greatest, I'm the best"—which is basically stupid.

That is exactly the situation in today's Gospel. Jesus was on a journey with his disciples, away from the crowds, since he wanted to make clear to them, personally, something important.

To start with, of course, what he was trying to say to them was quite incomprehensible. For he was talking about the dreadful suffering that lay ahead, about his violent death, and also about the way he would not remain dead but would rise again.

Instead of asking Jesus what it all meant, they lacked the confidence to do so. Perhaps they still did not want to understand it, since they would then have had to change their attitude and their lives. They would much rather have stayed with their power games, just for now . . . Later on, they did understand after all and followed Jesus' path, right to the point of being willing to put their lives on the line for him and for mankind.

For that is what it comes down to, that is what Jesus was trying to make clear to them, and what he himself lived out, to its final conclusion: the great person is not the one who makes himself important, the upwardly mobile person, but the one who learns how to serve. That looks impossible at first.

Yet among humans, the law of the strongest frequently dominates. Anyone who wants to be something has to assert himself. You need elbows to succeed. But is that really true?

Is not the best leader the one who is genuinely concerned for his colleagues? Is it not that business in which there is a sound, strong collective ambience which is successful, not the one in which there is a "pecking order" that spoils any joy and zest? Is it not those parents who are not solely centered on themselves and their success but accompany their children through life who are truly loved (and successful)?

Jesus pointed the way out of our own pompousness; he set a child in the midst of everyone and put his arms round him, as if he were trying to say, "Forget your own importance; look at children and grow simpler and less complicated! Accept one another just as I have taken this child in my arms! Perhaps we ought to talk about that as we walk along and not about who is the greatest."

TWENTY-SIXTH SUNDAY IN ORDINARY TIME

The Gospel of Mark 9:38–43, 45, 47–48

John said to him, "Teacher, we saw a man casting out demons in your name, and we forbade him, because he was not following us." But Jesus said, "Do not forbid him; for no one who does a mighty work in my name will be able soon after to speak evil of me. For he that is not against us is for us. For truly, I say to you, whoever gives you a cup of water to drink because you bear the name of Christ, will by no means lose his reward.

"Whoever causes one of these little ones who believe in me to sin, it would be better for him if a great millstone were hung round his neck and he were thrown into the sea. And if your hand causes you to sin, cut it off; it is better for you to enter life maimed than with two hands to go to hell, to the unquenchable fire. And if your foot causes you to sin, cut it off; it is better for you to enter life lame than with two feet to be thrown into hell. And if your eye causes you to sin, pluck it out; it is better for you to enter the kingdom of God with one eye than with two eyes to be thrown into hell, where their worm does not die, and the fire is not quenched."

Fighting and Tolerance

A difficult gospel reading that seems to contradict itself. Broad-minded and tolerant at the beginning and then radical, almost fanatically strict. Whenever we meet this kind of extreme contrast in Jesus' words, it means that the Master is trying to wake us up. To shake us into wakefulness, he uses strong language and striking images that we cannot ignore, that are bound to shake us. Let us try to be wide awake as we look at and listen to this and to see what refers to us in these words.

The first part talks about being open-minded and tolerant, and the second about what is intolerable and has therefore to be opposed with all our might.

One of the apostles, good old John, gets worked up about the way someone is doing good in the name of Jesus without belonging to "us", coming along "with us", being "one of us". He wants to forbid him to do this, to stop him. Jesus disapproves of that kind of attitude; in fact, he rejects it.

That is something his disciples, Christians, ought never to forget: there is a great deal of good even outside their circles. The boundaries of the Church are not Jesus' limits. You find so much readiness to help, so much kindness and love for one's neighbor, even outside the Church community. And wherever some good is done, there people are close to Jesus, and he to them. Even if they have only given an ordinary glass of water to someone who is thirsty, God will reward them for it.

You ought not to prevent anything that is good, but you should be tough on evil, merciless, especially against the evil within yourselves. This is where Jesus' tolerance is at an end. There is hardly anywhere where he speaks as sharply as he does here. The saying about the millstone around someone's neck shows what is truly intolerable in Jesus' view, where "zero tolerance" is appropriate. Better to get rid of your eye, your hand, or your foot than to give in to evil. Better to be saved with one eye, one hand, or one foot than to perish everlastingly with two.

What Jesus finds intolerable is tempting someone to do wrong. We are quite rightly furious today when we see how young people are being tempted to use drugs. It is quite right that child abuse, wherever it occurs, be sharply condemned. People are very much united on that point. But tempting people to do wrong can take many other forms: if prejudices are handed on from parents to children, for instance, or hate or hardhearted attitudes; or whenever bad and unfair working conditions undermine people's morale and make it all but impossible to live a decent life.

We have to fight against that.

But most especially against the temptation to do wrong that is lurking within my own self: we should be ruthless in taking steps against that. Rather cut your hand off than do wrong with it. Tear your foot off rather than walk along evil paths. Above all, however, look to your eye. Most temptation to evil comes from your eyes. I should add: and also from your tongue, which sows evil with words.

Jesus talks about hell. The danger of damnation lies within me. If I do not start with myself, in my fight against evil, that can bring me to a bad end. It is not against other people that I should be unyielding and intolerant, but against the inclination to evil within myself. In that fight, thank God, I am not alone: God is on my side!

The Gospel of Mark 10:2–16

And Pharisees came up and in order to test him asked, "Is it lawful for a man to divorce his wife?" He answered them, "What did Moses command you?" They said, "Moses allowed a man to write a certificate of divorce, and to put her away." But Jesus said to them, "For your hardness of heart he wrote you this commandment. But from the beginning of creation, 'God made them male and female.' 'For this reason a man shall leave his father and mother and be joined to his wife, and the two shall become one flesh.' So they are no longer two but one flesh. What therefore God has joined together, let not man put asunder."

And in the house the disciples asked him again about this matter. And he said to them, "Whoever divorces his wife and marries another, commits adultery against her; and if she divorces her husband and marries another, she commits adultery."

And they were bringing children to him, that he might touch them; and the disciples rebuked them. But when Jesus saw it he was indignant, and said to them, "Let the children come to me, do not hinder them; for to such belongs the kingdom of God. Truly, I say to you, whoever does not receive the kingdom of God like a child shall not enter it." And he took them in his arms and blessed them, laying his hands upon them.

❧

Becoming One Flesh

There is nothing new about the fact that marriage can be difficult. What is to be done when it just is not working any more? Do you have to stay together at all costs? Is there no way out, when marriage no longer seems to offer any way forward?

They wanted to test Jesus, to put him on the spot, to trap him: "Is a man allowed to divorce his wife?" What does Jesus say about divorce? And the question in response was, "What does the Bible say about it?" The Bible—here, it was the Old Testament—allowed a man to leave his wife. Not in any way at all, not simply by rejecting her, dismissing her, and leaving her defenseless; but it was permitted to establish a "writ of divorce". That was progress, in those days.

This gave the woman some degree of protection, and she was not turned onto the street with no rights at all. Yet the man still retained the advantage, for he could "dismiss" his wife, but she could not do that to him. A great deal has changed since then in divorce law. The protective clauses have been improved. And yet, there is still much pain and sorrow. A divorce usually leaves deep wounds behind it for both partners and still more often for the children.

So divorce was allowed in those days. Moses himself, who had written down God's laws, gave instructions for it.

Jesus, however, sees it all differently. He explains that what Moses prescribed was only a temporary solution to a difficulty. Because you are so hardhearted, so irreconcilable, he laid down this rule about divorce. That is certainly not God's will and plan. And then Jesus explains what God's original intention was: He created man and woman for each other, and they leave their parents so as to come together and to "be one flesh".

"One flesh": that means in the first instance the sexual union of the two of them. That is something God intends, and it is therefore good. It is not something illicit, still less evil.

Yet becoming "one flesh" means something more than merely sexual union. It means growing together, so that the two people become increasingly "one in heart and soul".

And Jesus says that God himself brings into being between the two people this process of "becoming one". God has united them. He has sealed their union. That is why the marital union is no longer the property of the two partners, at their disposal; it is more than a contract that can be dissolved again at will. "What therefore God has joined, let not man put asunder." And Jesus leaves us in no doubt about it: Anyone who leaves his spouse and marries someone else "commits adultery".

Even at the time, his followers were shocked by this strict attitude. Who would ever dare to marry if marriage is completely indissoluble? Something may always go wrong in life. Has Jesus no heart for those people whose relationship has broken down?

We do not find any place in the Gospel where Jesus condemns those people who have in some way or other come to grief in their lives. There is only one thing that he always condemns: hardness of heart. It is not failure that is so bad; it is behaving as if one had not failed. Someone who was sorry for the way he had failed was never dismissed by Jesus. And that, too, is something Jesus has always demanded of us: readiness to be reconciled. Would not many divorces be avoided if we had hardened our hearts less? And as if Jesus intended to touch our hearts, just after the discussion on divorce, he says, "Let the children come to me." Who is it who suffers most from any divorce? Jesus points to the children; he takes them in his arms and blesses them. Is this touching picture not an invitation to think again about divorce, with a view to the children?

The Gospel of Mark 10:17–27

A man ran up and knelt before [Jesus], and asked him, "Good Teacher, what must I do to inherit eternal life?" And Jesus said to him, "Why do you call me good? No one is good but God alone. You know the commandments: 'Do not kill, Do not commit adultery, Do not steal, Do not bear false witness, Do not defraud, Honor your father and mother.'" And he said to him, "Teacher, all these I have observed from my youth." And Jesus looking upon him loved him, and said to him, "You lack one thing; go, sell what you have, and give to the poor, and you will have treasure in heaven; and come, follow me." At that saying his countenance fell, and he went away sorrowful; for he had great possessions.

And Jesus looked around and said to his disciples, "How hard it will be for those who have riches to enter the kingdom of God!" And the disciples were amazed at his words. But Jesus said to them again, "Children, how hard it is for those who trust in riches to enter the kingdom of God! It is easier for a camel to go through the eye of a needle than for a rich man to enter the kingdom of God." And they were exceedingly astonished, and said to him, "Then who can be saved?" Jesus looked at them and said, "With men it is impossible, but not with God; for all things are possible with God."

છે

The Camel and the Eye of the Needle

A rich man comes to Jesus with the great question in his life: "What must I do to achieve eternal life?" I wonder: Is that the question that really concerns us today?

In those days, in past times, it may well have been many people's most pressing concern in their lives: How do I get to heaven? How do I make sure of achieving the ultimate goal of my life? What do I have to do for that?

Am I mistaken in my impression that with us, nowadays, it is mostly other questions that are in the forefront: How can I succeed in my life in this world? How can I be happy, here and now? We put off until later asking about what comes afterward, after death, or we push it out of our field of vision altogether. The main thing is what suits our present life! Or is the question about eternal life raised more often than apparently seems to be the case?

It is of course surprising that Jesus does not seem especially pleased about the rich man's pious question. His answer is brusque and brief: "Why call me good? Only God is good!" What was for the rich man an expression of respect ("Good Master") Jesus brusquely refuses to accept: "Don't look for any kind of 'master' who might be able to show you special, secret ways to achieve eternal happiness." The way to it has long ago been shown to us by God, quite clearly so that anyone can understand it: You need only keep the Ten Commandments. They will assuredly lead you to the goal of eternal life.

We like to look for special ways, secret recipes, for attaining happiness, and to that end we chase after all kinds of health gurus and people who teach us how to live and expect goodness knows what kind of advice from them to find the key to happiness. Jesus offers us no secret recipe; he is not the "miracle doctor" by whom we might hope to be offered (at a high price) the solution to our own problems. The only thing he has ready for us are these simple words: "The thing that is God's will, and the only thing that makes us happy, is something each person knows in his own heart: God's commandments."

He has been trying to do that from his youth, the rich man replies. Now Jesus himself is touched. He looks at him lovingly and invites him to take the one step that is still lacking: Let go! Let go of your riches, give everything to the poor, and come with me! Yet the rich man cannot bring himself to take this step.

What comes next is a complete reversal of the way we currently see things. Anyone who wins millions in a lottery is regarded as happy. Anyone numbered among the super-rich is doing well. Anyone who can have anything he wants is envied. No. For Jesus, it is exactly the opposite. Just as an enormous camel cannot possibly push its way through the eye of a needle, so a rich man cannot possibly get into heaven.

The disciples are as horrified as we are hearing this today. But Jesus makes it mercilessly clear: You cannot get through the gate of death with your enormous baggage of wealth. You have to let go of everything; you can take nothing with you except the good that you have done in your lifetime.

That is why Jesus advises the rich man to let go of everything now and not wait until death, when it will be too late to do it of your own free will. "But that is humanly impossible", complain the disciples. "No one can manage to let go so completely." "Oh, yes", replies Jesus, "It is possible with God."

The Gospel of Mark 10:35–45

And James and John, the sons of Zebedee, came forward to him, and said to him, "Teacher, we want you to do for us whatever we ask of you." And he said to them, "What do you want me to do for you?" And they said to him, "Grant us to sit, one at your right hand and one at your left, in your glory." But Jesus said to them, "You do not know what you are asking. Are you able to drink the chalice that I drink, or to be baptized with the baptism with which I am baptized?" And they said to him, "We are able." And Jesus said to them, the chalice that I drink you will drink; and with the baptism with which I am baptized, you will be baptized; but to sit at my right hand or at my left is not mine to grant, but it is for those for whom it has been prepared." And when the ten heard it, they began to be indignant at James and John. And Jesus called them to him and said to them, "You know that those who are supposed to rule over the Gentiles lord it over them, and their great men exercise authority over them. But it shall not be so among you; but whoever would be great among you must be your servant, and whoever would be first among you must be slave of all. For the Son of man also came not to be served but to serve, and to give his life as a ransom for many."

A Downward Career

Rarely has it been clear and tangible to so many people how true Jesus' saying is, "Whoever would be great among you must be your servant", as it was in the case of Blessed Mother Teresa of Calcutta (1910–1997). She made herself a "downward career", so to speak. She was not forever climbing higher; she was forever going lower down. She came down from the well-respected position of a member of a religious order, who was a good teacher in a good convent school, to the poorest of the poor, those who were dying in the streets of Calcutta. In doing so she was following the path of Jesus, who "came not to be served but to serve", to the point of being prepared to give his own life.

Hardly anyone in the world was as popular and beloved among both Christians and non-Christians as this little woman. What is so attractive about her? Why is her "downward" path so fascinating for many people?

Perhaps because we all feel, in our hearts, that this is the better path to take and that it makes people happier than the one being talked about in today's Gospel reading. There was a minor crisis among the twelve apostles, which Jesus handled marvelously well. They had been the first people Jesus had called, and nothing is easier to understand, from the human point of view, than the way they concluded from this that they were better and more important than the others who came later. Two pairs of brothers, Simon Peter and Andrew and James and John, fishermen from the Lake of Gennesaret, had been the first to be called.

Now that things were getting serious, with Jesus talking time and again about his end, his death, they probably thought they would have to make provision for the future, and quickly. They did not know how it would all turn out with Jesus, but they hoped he would set up the "kingdom of God", a marvelous realm in which everything would be made new and good and in which they wanted to make sure they got the best places, the positions of most power.

It is almost touching how honestly James and John admitted their ambition. And it is not surprising that the other ten were annoyed by this careerist attitude. That is just the way things usually go in our world (and also, unfortunately, in the Church). Jesus, however, shows them a different and greater career—not only in words, but by his example: "If you want to be really close to me, then you have to walk along the way with me, the way of the Cross; you have to drink the cup of suffering with me and accept the baptism of death."

And again, it is touching how spontaneously both of them said, "We are ready to do that." All twelve did in fact later follow Jesus to the point of martyrdom, without hesitation.

"Become little, like children", says Jesus again and again; "do not make yourselves out to be great, like powerful people": Service makes you great—that is what Mother Teresa shows us. "Love", she never stops saying (and giving us by her example), "Love till it hurts."

———

The Gospel of Mark 10:46–52

And [Jesus and his disciples] came to Jericho; and as he was leaving Jericho with his disciples and a great multitude, Bartimaeus, a blind beggar, the son of Timaeus, was sitting by the roadside. And when he heard that it was Jesus of Nazareth, he began to cry out and say, "Jesus, Son of David, have mercy on me!" And many rebuked him, telling him to be silent; but he cried out all the more, "Son of David, have mercy on me!" And Jesus stopped and said, "Call him." And they called the blind man, saying to him, "Take heart; rise, he is calling you." And throwing off his cloak he sprang up and came to Jesus. And Jesus said to him, "What do you want me to do for you?" And the blind man said to him, "Master, let me receive my sight." And Jesus said to him, "Go your way; your faith has made you well." And immediately he received his sight and followed him on the way.

༄

Thanks, Bartimaeus!

Anyone who has been in the poor countries of the world— and that includes most countries—is used to the sight of blind beggars. In addition to miserable poverty, they have blindness to cope with. That makes them even more helpless. Nowadays, a good many cases of blindness can be prevented in those countries with better medical care. Aid organizations such as the Christoffel Blind Mission do marvelous work. Nonetheless, the high rate of blindness remains one of the typical characteristics of the poorest countries. Jesus' native land was among them. That is why we meet so many blind people in the Gospels.

But we know the name of only one of them: Bartimaeus, the son of Timaeus. His cry for help is like the echo of so many who are poor and blind. Yet it is also the echo of a spiritual need. How many people are sitting at the roadside of life—alone in their helplessness, pushed to one side, seen as a burden—whose cry for help people would like to silence because it disturbs other people's rest or enjoyment. Bartimaeus could be my neighbor.

What moves us about the blind man of Jericho is that he does not let himself be just "got rid of". He cries his misery aloud. He cannot be made to keep silent. Anyone who is despairing is silent. Anyone who calls for help is still hoping. Bartimaeus touches us because he is still hoping. He may rekindle the spark of hope in me, too. He shows what can happen.

Bartimaeus hears that it is on account of Jesus that such a crowd is collecting on the road that leads up to Jerusalem. He has heard of Jesus, as so many people had at that time. He can work miracles, he has heard, heal sick people; he has even helped some hopeless cases. Who knows whether he might even be able to help me? And so Bartimaeus calls Jesus by name, cries out for him, to get a hearing in this dense crowd. He calls louder and louder, until finally Jesus, whom he is calling, stops and calls him to his side.

How typical the crowd's behavior is: first they want to silence the person who is calling out and making a nuisance of himself; then—in a complete about-face—they encourage the blind man to hurry to Jesus. So-called public opinion is, after all, much like a weather vane. It also does me good to look in this mirror and to ask myself how easy it is for me sometimes to think and act one way and then, right afterward, in another way altogether.

Now, however, the crowd is of no further interest. Jesus and the blind man meet, and only their meeting counts: "What do you want me to do for you?" "Rabboni, dear Master, let me receive my sight."

The hope that Jesus can heal me, too, my sick body and still more my sick soul, is the gift to us of this blind man on the roadside near Jericho. Since the day when he cried out loud for help, creating a disturbance, that cry has never been silent. At each Holy Mass, his plea is repeated: "Lord, have mercy upon us!" His trust is catching. Following his example, anyone, in whatever kind of trouble, can call out to Jesus. Thank you, Bartimaeus, for not letting anyone stop you from hoping in Jesus!

The Gospel of Mark 12:28b–34

And one of the scribes came up and . . . asked him, "Which commandment is the first of all?" Jesus answered, "The first is, 'Hear, O Israel: The Lord our God, the Lord is one; and you shall love the Lord your God with all your heart, and with all your soul, and with all your mind, and with all your strength.' The second is this, 'You shall love your neighbor as yourself.' There is no other commandment greater than these." And the scribe said to him, "You are right, Teacher; you have truly said that he is one, and there is no other but he; and to love him with all the heart, and with all the understanding, and with all the strength, and to love one's neighbor as oneself, is much more than all whole burnt offerings and sacrifices." And when Jesus saw that he answered wisely, he said to him, "You are not far from the kingdom of God." And after that no one dared to ask him any question.

God's Deputy

There are so many commandments. Judaism reckons it as over six hundred in the Old Testament. Are they all equally important? Of course not. Yet how can we weigh up their seriousness? Which are the really urgent ones, and which are less significant? Or, do they all have to be observed with the same care? Which are really God's commandments, and which ones are human inventions that have been added? The more we have to observe laws made by men, the more difficult it becomes to "filter out" which are God's own commandments.

It is vitally necessary to keep God's commandments. His commandments are the paths of life, and they are intended to warn us against "paths of death". God is a friend to life, Old Testament wisdom says. He does not desire our destruction, our death, but that we should live. That is why it is so vitally important to know his commandments and to live in accordance with them.

In order that we may not fail to live up to them, God has inscribed his commandments in our hearts. God's fundamental commandments, as recorded in the Ten Commandments, the Decalogue, which God passed on to Moses on Mount Sinai, are not imposed upon us from without, as if they were arbitrary, alien instructions. We find them in our conscience, the most intimate voice of God in our hearts. We do not actually need to learn them. Every child knows them through the moral instinct that is alive within him.

If the hundreds of commandments we find in the Bible can all be seen as deriving from the Ten Commandments, then we may still ask which of these Ten is the most important. Sometimes we get the impression that the well-known Sixth Commandment is the most important, with the theme of sexuality so much in the forefront as the "number-one subject".

Jesus' reply to the scribe is so clear and logical that we can only wonder why it is that it is not so clear in life. The most important commandment is the first of the Ten. It sums them all up, and it alone makes it possible for us to fulfill the others.

Dieu premier servi was the motto of Saint Joan of Orléans (Jeanne d'Arc, 1412–1431): "Serve God first of all!"—but not in the sense that we divide up our service by percentages: so much for God, the rest for other people and other things. Jesus—along with the Old Testament—is quite clear about this. It has to be 100 percent: loving God "with all your heart, and with all your soul, and with all your mind, and with all your strength". There are no exceptions. Everything has to be entirely and unconditionally "invested" in loving God.

If God is God, this is quite clear. Then he is the First and the Last, the alpha and omega of our life. If that is so, then why is it often so little true in our lives? Why does God often come last in my life? Why do I turn to him only when all else has failed? Why is he so often no more than a stopgap, even in the lives of pious Christians? Because we are (still) so far from our goal! Because we far too much set ourselves at the center of things instead of God. The First Commandment is the most important. That is the goal we want to reach if we want to have full, whole, and happy lives.

And how do we get there? Jesus mentions it in the same breath as the First Commandment: "You shall love your neighbor as yourself." We are led on to a greater love of God, day by day, by patiently following the path of loving our neighbor. Our neighbor is "God's deputy", and by loving him we learn to love, with our whole heart and with all our strength, him who stands behind our neighbor.

————

The Gospel of Mark 12:41–44

[Jesus] sat down opposite the treasury, and watched the multitude putting money into the treasury. Many rich people put in large sums. And a poor widow came, and put in two copper coins, which make a penny. And he called his disciples to him, and said to them, "Truly, I say to you, this poor widow has put in more than all those who are contributing to the treasury. For they all contributed out of their abundance; but she out of her poverty has put in everything she had, her whole living."

৯৯

What Matters to Jesus

We are almost at the end of the Church's year. In a certain sense, today's Gospel represents the end of Jesus' public teaching and ministry. This little scene in the temple at Jerusalem is something like a conclusion to the Gospel, the briefest possible summary of it. After that, Jesus goes on to talk at length about the "last things", which will precede his return. Then follows the story of his Passion, beginning at the Last Supper and ending with the empty tomb.

Let us follow Jesus into the temple at Jerusalem, which he already loved so much as a child that in talking to his parents, who had been looking for him anxiously, he called it "my Father's house". He is passionately committed to the cause of this earthly "house of my Father". The drastic way he cleanses the temple is evidence of the way he cares about the purity and holiness of the temple, which is not to be allowed to become merely a "house of trade" or a "den of robbers" (Mk 11:15–19).

He often teaches there in the temple, holds disputations, and above all prays (even though this is not mentioned explicitly). We see him there today, just sitting and watching people as they crowd into the temple. He has chosen a particular spot, "opposite the treasury", the great "offertory box" of the temple. He "watched the multitude putting money into the treasury".

His gaze falls on a "poor widow", who "put in two copper coins". What strikes us about Jesus? First, his gaze! Jesus sits and looks. Becoming a disciple of Jesus means, in the first place, learning to look at things the way he looks at them. His way of looking at things should become ours. Unless we learn to see people, things, and situations with his eyes, then we have not yet become his disciples.

Where are his disciples during this scene? They must have come into the temple with him. He is on his own. Their eyes, their attention are (yet again) somewhere else. They seem to find something else more interesting. Thus, Jesus first has to call them together. The Greek word that the evangelist Mark uses here comes from the same root as the word for "church". The Church is "called together", the congregation of those people whom God, Christ, brings together around him by his call. He makes dispersed, distracted people into collected people (in both senses of the word). We humans go our own way, each for himself, and are often somehow spiritually "scattered". Jesus calls people together, he gathers them, so that they themselves become "collected".

So Jesus calls his disciples together. He has to show them something to which they have been paying no attention, something really important, even decisive: the poor widow. What is there to see, apart from her poverty? Something that only Jesus has noticed, because his gaze never halts at externals: she has put more than anyone else into the offertory box—she has put everything she has, all she has to live on: literally, "her whole life".

That is exactly what Jesus wants to show them. Jesus sets before his disciples this widow, who has given everything to God. In her selfless sacrifice, Jesus sees a summary of his whole gospel. "Blessed are the poor in spirit, for theirs is the kingdom of heaven" (Mt 5:3, literally). The poor widow is doing what Jesus is soon going to do: give his life for us completely. If Jesus' disciples do not overlook her, if their eyes are alert to the poor and the little people, they will also understand what is Jesus' inmost concern, what really matters to Jesus.

The Gospel of Mark 13:24–32

[*Jesus said to his disciples,*] *"But in those days, after that tribulation, the sun will be darkened, and the moon will not give its light, and the stars will be falling from heaven, and the powers in the heavens will be shaken. And then they will see the Son of man coming in clouds with great power and glory. And then he will send out the angels, and gather his elect from the four winds, from the ends of the earth to the ends of heaven.*

"From the fig tree learn its lesson: as soon as its branch becomes tender and puts forth its leaves, you know that summer is near. So also, when you see these things taking place, you know that he is near, at the very gates. Truly, I say to you, this generation will not pass away before all these things take place. Heaven and earth will pass away, but my words will not pass away.

"But of that day or that hour no one knows, not even the angels in heaven, nor the Son, but only the Father."

End of the World

I am sometimes struck by a strange thought: there will come a time when my beloved Cathedral of Saint Stephen in Vienna will no longer exist. I hope, as do we all, that it will be there for a long, long time. It is already more than 850 years old. May it stand for another thousand years! Yet sometime, everything on earth will come to an end. "Heaven and earth will pass away."

Nowadays the scientists tell us that our universe, this unimaginably enormous cosmos, began at a point in the past, maybe fourteen billion years ago, and that at some time, in billions of years, it will come to an end. The brief history of our earth represents only a tiny fraction of the duration of the universe. It is certain that we will come to an end. It is certain that the earth, the sun, our galaxy, indeed, the entire universe, will reach the end of their lives one day. The scientists can tell us roughly when that will be for the cosmos: in a few billion years.

We do not feel affected by that, because the time spans are so astronomically vast. Concerning our own earthly pilgrimage, on the other hand, we cannot know when "the day and the hour" will come. It could be today or not for years. It is certain only that one day, I, too, will come to that.

For Jesus, the hour has come. Today's Gospel reading tells about his last days in Jerusalem, shortly before the drama of the crucifixion. And Jesus is talking to his disciples about the "last days of the human race", about the end of time on earth. But when will all that happen? Is the end right around the corner? Are there signs to tell us, indicators, so to speak, whose flashing will alert us that the last hour has come?

Jesus himself lays down a hard-and-fast rule: Nobody knows the hour! So there is the end to speculation about the end of the world! Only God knows when that will be. He alone is Master of time and Lord of the universe. "Infinite thy vast domain", we sing, in "Holy God We Praise Thy Name". No one, not even Jesus himself, can specify the time. Jesus could do so, but he does not want to, since it has to be clear that that is the business of God [the Father] alone.

If that is how it is, then why worry about the end? We can

do nothing about, it, after all. Well, certainly, but we can at any rate make our contribution, for better or for worse. And at the moment we are busy making things worse, all over the world . . . Global warming, the destruction of the "lungs of the earth", the tropical rain forests, the squandering of natural energy reserves, and many other things that do not actually bring about the end of the world, yet nonetheless inflict lasting damage to life on earth.

We have to recognize the seriousness of the situation. Worse than the external threat to the environment is the spiritual damage being done. There is a miniature "end of the world" if my own world collapses, if relationships break down or jobs are lost. How fragile is human life! Things that look so safe seem to be threatened. In the autumn, the whole of nature reminds us how things pass away. "My words will not pass away", says Jesus. We can hold fast to him. When everything else is tottering, he still remains.

CHRIST THE KING

The Gospel of John 18:33–37

Pilate . . . called Jesus, and said to him, "Are you the King of the Jews?" Jesus answered, "Do you say this of your own accord, or did others say it to you about me?" Pilate answered, "Am I a Jew? Your own nation and the chief priests have handed you over to me; what have you done?" Jesus answered, "My kingship is not of this world; if my kingship were of this world, my servants would fight, that I might not be handed over to the Jews; but my kingship is not from the world." Pilate said to him, "So you are a king?" Jesus answered, "You say that I am a king. For this I was born, and for this I have come into the world, to bear witness to the truth. Every one who is of the truth hears my voice."

ॐ

This Mirror

"Yes, I am a king." The man who says this is standing powerless and in chains before the emperor's deputy. What a contrast! What can this powerless king achieve in the history of the world?

Power, after all, is to be found somewhere else entirely, in the positions of political and economic administration, where the great of this world call the shots. This man, who is standing before Pilate as a prisoner, has no army behind him, no massive financial backing, no political power. By human standards, he ought to have been long forgotten, swallowed up in the broad stream of history.

But he is still there. He is still standing before the powerful people of this world. Each of us has some little desire to be one of the powerful people, if only at home or at work, in front of our colleagues, as compared with other people. Jesus stands before me as he did before Pilate, the little provincial governor who liked to underline the fact that he was a great man; and his conversation with Pilate becomes a mirror that Jesus is holding up to me: What do you look like? Are you living by appearances or by the truth? Do I dare to look into this mirror?

Pilate asks Jesus, "Who are you? Are you the King of the Jews?"

The question with which Jesus responds holds a mirror up to him: "Do you say this of your own accord, or did others say it to you about me?"

Are you saying that because that is the "general opinion"? Or are you saying it because you really want to know for yourself? Are you under pressure, because "other people" are persuading you to say it, or does the question come from your heart?

Look in the mirror: How many of my views are mere prejudices? How much of what I think and say is what I have simply taken over from "other people", without asking myself whether I really think it myself?

I am always hurt when I find, time and again, how thoughtlessly people pass on even prejudices against the Church without checking them. We ought to try to let ourselves be influenced as little as possible by prejudice. We should ask, again and again, "Is this my personal opinion, which I have arrived at through knowledge of the facts, or am I just repeating 'what other people have said'?"

Pilate is made uncomfortable by Jesus' question. He is not prepared to look in the mirror that Jesus is holding up to him: "Am I a Jew? What have you done?" Jesus' reply is on a quite different level: "My kingship is not of this world." If my kingship were a worldly one, then my followers would fight on my behalf.

Again, here is a mirror: Not only this world exists; there is also the other world, beyond death. The powerful people of this world do not hold sway over the other world. There are limits to their power. All earthly power is limited. In the last century we found by experience where it leads when dictators and totalitarian states try to dominate men's souls as well. Anyone who accepts Christ as his King cannot be subjugated. Christ will liberate him. The King who stands before Pilate in chains sets people free from all the bonds of self-deception and lies. Only one thing is needed: an honest striving for the truth. Look in this mirror!

Lent

and

the Easter Season

The Gospel of Mark 1:12–15

The Spirit immediately drove [Jesus] out into the wilderness. And he was in the wilderness forty days, tempted by Satan; and he was with the wild beasts; and the angels ministered to him.

Now after John was arrested, Jesus came into Galilee, preaching the gospel of God, and saying, "The time is fulfilled, and the kingdom of God is at hand; repent, and believe in the gospel."

๛

The Wilderness Blossoms

It could not be more succinct. Mark the Evangelist devotes only a few lines to Jesus' forty days in the wilderness. These forty days are the model for the forty days of Lent, which begins on Ash Wednesday. What did Jesus intend, with his time in the wilderness? What was it like for him? What is the model that the Christian season of Lent is meant to imitate?

The information Mark gives is so sparing that it is difficult to answer these questions. Yet when we look closer, we find that these few words are densely packed with content.

First, the point in time: Jesus had just had himself baptized in the Jordan by John the Baptist. This was the outset of his ministry. Hitherto he had lived a quite unremarkable life as an artisan. At around thirty years of age he suddenly left all this. He went to John and simply lined up among all the people who were coming to confess their sins and to let themselves be immersed in the water as a sign of repentance and of a new beginning. Right from the start, Jesus set himself in the midst of people. That was why he had come. "Those who are well have no need of a physician, but those who are sick; I came not to call the righteous, but sinners" (Mk 2:17) was the way he would later explain his task. And that is exactly what the people were, among whom Jesus took his place at the Jordan: sinners, sick in body and soul. And he saw his task as that of making them well again. Words, mere talking, was of no help here. Jesus went to the root of the evil. That was why he went into the wilderness, where God's Spirit drove him.

The wilderness is hard to endure. The Jewish people knew that from their memory of the forty years in the wilderness. All external props are removed—no entertainment, no fun. Silence and solitude. Enduring the wilderness alone for forty days is a hard test in itself.

Yet in that time, Jesus was "tempted by Satan", besides. In addition to the outward struggle for life, there came the inner torment of temptation. Of what did this consist? Nowadays, we mostly think straightaway of sexual allurements, and of nothing else. They are there, and they are not easy to fight against. Other temptations may strike deeper: those of meaninglessness and despair, of boasting and being in control—and finally the most radical temptation, that of turning away from God.

How did Jesus experience these temptations? We do not know. But he did withstand them, and he did so not simply for himself, but also on our behalf. At the beginning, there was his fight against the temptations of the devil. In those forty days, Jesus was fighting on our behalf. It was a representative struggle, so to speak. He was trying to help us, not merely with fine words, but by taking our struggle upon himself. He can heal us and help us only if he knows "whereof we are made", how frail we are, and what easy prey we often are for Satan, the tempter. Jesus took up the fight for us, and he was victorious.

Mark shows this victory by two signs: Jesus lives in the wilderness "with the wild beasts". They do not harm him, there is peace among them, because he is at peace with God. We know, from the lives of many saints, that they lived in harmony with the animal kingdom like this. And "the angels ministered" to Jesus: yet another image of peace, not only with the realm of animal life, but also with the heavenly realm. Because Jesus has overcome evil and the devil, peace emanates from him. The wilderness becomes a paradise.

Jesus intends that peace should come into our wildernesses when he exhorts us to "repent, and believe in the gospel."

The Gospel of Mark 9:2–10

And after six days Jesus took with him Peter and James and John, and led them up a high mountain apart by themselves; and he was transfigured before them, and his garments became glistening, intensely white, as no fuller on earth could bleach them. And there appeared to them Elijah with Moses; and they were talking to Jesus. And Peter said to Jesus, "Master, it is well that we are here; let us make three booths, one for you and one for Moses and one for Elijah." For he did not know what to say, for they were exceedingly afraid. And a cloud overshadowed them, and a voice came out of the cloud, "This is my beloved Son; listen to him." And suddenly looking around they no longer saw any one with them but Jesus only.

And as they were coming down the mountain, he charged them to tell no one what they had seen, until the Son of man should have risen from the dead. So they kept the matter to themselves, questioning what the rising from the dead meant.

The Path of Transfiguration

Even up on a high mountain, silence is a rarity nowadays. There is almost always some noise to be heard, up from the valleys or out of the sky, from airplanes on their unceasing course. Silence has become a rare and precious commodity.

158

Jesus frequently sought out silence, withdrew on his own to a mountain to pray. As he does in today's Gospel reading. He rarely took anyone else with him, as he does this time.

Among the twelve apostles, three—the three allowed to climb up to the solitude of the mountain with him—were especially close to him: Peter and the brothers James and John. They would be with him at another hour of solitude—more asleep than awake, of course—among the olive trees in the garden of Gethsemane on the night when he was troubled, "sorrowful even to death", and when he was arrested.

What they experienced in the silence on the mountain was something quite different, something unique. Jesus was transfigured before their eyes. Everything was bathed in light—or, more precisely, light began to stream forth from Jesus, from his clothing and from his face. They struggled to find some comparison for this: it was whiter than any white clothing could ever be.

There was something else, besides the manifestation of light. They saw next to Jesus the two most important figures from the Old Testament, Moses and Elijah. And they heard a voice from heaven, bearing witness to Jesus as Son of God. This experience must have been so tremendous and so blissful that they would have liked to hold on to it. But it remained just an unforgettable moment.

There are two questions: How can we picture this unique event for ourselves? And why do we read about it on the second Sunday of Lent?

We may get some idea of it when we think about the times we have come across people who are "radiant"—radiant with happiness, with joy—or when people seem to us "transfigured" in suffering, in old age, even in death.

This scene is called the "Transfiguration of Jesus". It does happen that people begin to shine, as if from within. I have met one such unbelievably radiant person, Franziska Jägerstätter. She has had to bear great suffering. Her husband was beheaded on August 9, 1943, by Hitler's henchmen, because he was not prepared, on account of his faith, to serve in Hitler's war. Her life has been, as she herself said, "one long Good Friday". Yet her strong, deep faith has not allowed her to grow bitter. Anyone who meets her can feel something of what the three apostles may have experienced on the mount of the Transfiguration.

And that likewise explains why this Gospel is read in Lent, particularly. The point of these forty days of penitence is to draw nearer to God. "God is light", says the Bible. Anyone who comes close to God in his heart, in his life, through faith, will himself become more luminous, become brighter, more like Jesus, who is God's beloved Son. The path to this may of course be steep, a way of the Cross. Yet at the end there is Easter, a radiant joy.

THIRD SUNDAY OF LENT

———

The Gospel of John 2:13–25

The Passover of the Jews was at hand, and Jesus went up to Jerusalem. In the temple he found those who were selling oxen and sheep and pigeons, and the money-changers at their business. And making a whip of cords, he drove them all, with the sheep and oxen, out of the temple; and he poured out the coins of the money-changers and overturned their tables. And he told those who sold the pigeons, "Take these things away; you shall not make my Father's house a house of trade." His disciples remembered that it was written, "Zeal for your house will consume me." The Jews then said to him, "What sign have you to show us for doing this?" Jesus answered them, "Destroy this temple, and in three days I will raise it up." The Jews then said, "It has taken forty-six years to build this temple, and will you raise it up in three days?" But he spoke of the temple of his body. When therefore he was raised from the dead, his disciples remembered that he had said this; and they believed the Scripture and the word which Jesus had spoken.

Now when he was in Jerusalem at the Passover feast, many believed in his name when they saw the signs which he did; but Jesus did not trust himself to them, because he knew all men and needed no one to bear witness of man; for he himself knew what was in man.

ع>

Cleansing the Temple Today

There are many days, in the Cathedral of Saint Stephen in Vienna, when the saying of Jesus that we have heard today comes to my mind, "Do not make God's house a house of trade!" Where is the sense of the holiness of this place? There is loud talking; many come in eating and drinking and are even abusive if a verger points out that this is inappropriate. Such behavior would be unthinkable in any mosque.

Jesus deeply loved the Jerusalem temple. He had been brought to the temple by Mary and Joseph as a newborn baby and probably came time and again for the many pilgrim feasts.

Once, as a twelve-year-old, he had remained there, and when his parents found their missing child in the temple, he asked them in astonishment, "Did you not know that I must be in my Father's house?" (Lk 2:49) For him, the temple was his Father's house, and that was why he felt at home there. That was also why he could not bear to have it turned into a house of trade—a "robbers' den", indeed.

Where God was concerned, or the poor, or honesty, Jesus could be far from peaceable. At some times he was seized by "a holy wrath". The cleansing of the temple is one such instance. This Gospel is read during Lent because it is something that needs pointing out even today, not only in the Cathedral of Saint Stephen or other churches that have many tourists visiting them, but above all within ourselves. For we are God's temple, and Jesus' "holy wrath" is set aflame by all the rubbish that has collected within us.

And just as Jesus used a whip to drive out of the temple all commercial activities, so he does not hesitate to make occasional use of strong means in our case, because it is his will

162

that our body and our soul be God's dwelling place and should not decline into robbers' dens.

The cords of the whip might for instance be the consequence of our mistakes and our sins that we have to suffer. They should help to expel from our lives much that is bad, so that we may once more be God's dwelling place.

How badly we need this "cleansing of the temple" is shown by the final remark in today's Gospel reading: Jesus "knew what was in man".

He knows us, knows whereof we are made and how incapable we are of expelling all the rubbish from our lives by our own efforts. That is why he takes the cleansing of the temple in hand himself.

The instrument he uses is the Cross, which he took upon himself on our behalf: "Destroy this temple", says Jesus—thereby referring to his body, which was killed on the Cross—and in three days, he says, he will "raise it up", he will rise from the dead.

The apostles first understood what that meant after it happened. And we can understand it if we accept many of the trials in our lives as being purifications. Jesus bore them for us. With him, there is a resurrection, a new life. Thus, "cleansing of the temple" is still happening today.

Gospel of John 3:14–21

[Then Jesus said to Nicodemus,] "As Moses lifted up the serpent in the wilderness, so must the Son of man be lifted up, that whoever believes in him may have eternal life."

For God so loved the world that he gave his only-begotten Son, that whoever believes in him should not perish but have eternal life. For God sent the Son into the world, not to condemn the world, but that the world might be saved through him. He who believes in him is not condemned; he who does not believe is condemned already, because he has not believed in the name of the only-begotten Son of God. And this is the judgment, that the light has come into the world, and men loved darkness rather than light, because their deeds were evil. For every one who does evil hates the light, and does not come to the light, lest his deeds should be exposed. But he who does what is true comes to the light, that it may be clearly seen that his deeds have been wrought in God.

Part of a Nighttime Conversation

Many conversations can be carried on better at night, when it is quiet outside and in, when the bustle of the day has died away. Then we can sometimes manage to put into words things that are really important and essential, to go more deeply into things than is possible in the daytime.

Nicodemus, a member of the council, comes to Jesus for that sort of conversation one night. Does he come at such a late hour because he is afraid of being seen and criticized for having any contact with this controversial Jesus from Galilee? Or is he looking for the silence of nighttime, when he might hope for quiet in which to talk about his deepest questionings to Jesus? Perhaps he is acting thus for both reasons, the way we often have various motives for what we do.

What is certain is that in this "Nicodemus hour" (which is what people in Austria still call this kind of very personal nighttime conversation) Jesus lets us see deep into the mystery of his own life.

In the first part of the conversation (before today's passage), Jesus makes it quite clear from the start that in order to attain life's goal, to enter the "kingdom of heaven", we have to be born anew "from above". Nicodemus does not understand that at all. An adult cannot, after all, become a baby once more, still less an embryo. For all his learning, Jesus' nighttime visitor does not understand what he means. It is a matter of being born again—not so as to live for as long as possible on this earth, but so as to have the kind of life that no death can destroy. Jesus says to Nicodemus that heaven and "eternal life" are to be had only if we undergo a new birth.

This is where today's Gospel begins: the second part of the nocturnal conversation. How can we get out of the rut of our old lives and find new life, eternal life? Jesus expresses it with an image from the Bible: Once, during their forty years of wandering through the wilderness, the Jews had been particularly rebellious against God's ways. They were attacked by a plague of poisonous serpents. Many of the Jews died. Moses made a metal serpent and set it up on high. Anyone who looked up at it was healed.

That is how we ought to act, Jesus advises Nicodemus.

Once he is hanging on the Cross on high, then we ought to look up to him, and looking at him will make us whole again and give us new life.

Looking up to the Cross! How often peace has stolen into our restless hearts, consolation in our despair, remorse, and readiness to stand up again, to begin again, to carry on! Many people can confirm that from their own experience.

Yet in this nighttime conversation, we also discover why it is that it helps so much to look up to the One who is crucified. In one of the loveliest sayings Jesus ever uttered, he says to Nicodemus—and through him, to us all—that God loves the world so much that he will do anything for it; he even gives up for us what is most precious to him, his Son. It becomes clear thereby that God wants, not to judge people, but to save them. Anyone who knows and believes that will not fall victim to the darkness, when everything is obscure and difficult. Jesus tells his nighttime visitor, "Believe in this love! It is stronger than anything else, even death!" We should take the time, now and then, for such a "Nicodemus hour" with Jesus.

But to believe in love also means to act accordingly. Jesus expresses this in the surprising turn of phrase "doing what is true". Words alone are not enough; love has to show itself in actions. If God has done so much for us, to the point of becoming man himself, so that we might not perish, then we ought likewise honestly and seriously to have as much time for one another as God has for us.

We ought perhaps occasionally to make time for ourselves, during Lent, to have just this kind of "Nicodemus hour" in the silence of the night.

———

The Gospel of John 12:20–33

Now among those who went up to worship at the feast were some Greeks. So these came to Philip, who was from Bethsaida in Galilee, and said to him, "Sir, we wish to see Jesus." Philip went and told Andrew; Andrew went with Philip and they told Jesus. And Jesus answered them, "The hour has come for the Son of man to be glorified. Truly, truly, I say to you, unless a grain of wheat falls into the earth and dies, it remains alone; but if it dies, it bears much fruit. He who loves his life loses it, and he who hates his life in this world will keep it for eternal life. If any one serves me, he must follow me; and where I am, there shall my servant be also; if any one serves me, the Father will honor him.

"Now is my soul troubled. And what shall I say? 'Father, save me from this hour'? No, for this purpose I have come to this hour. Father, glorify your name." Then a voice came from heaven, "I have glorified it, and I will glorify it again." The crowd standing by heard it and said that it had thundered. Others said, "An angel has spoken to him." Jesus answered, "This voice has come for your sake, not for mine. Now is the judgment of this world, now shall the ruler of this world be cast out; and I, when I am lifted up from the earth, will draw all men to myself." He said this to show by what death he was to die.

ও

Die and Live, Grain of Wheat!

Easter is coming. We can tell it by the spring air, and likewise by today's Gospel reading. The pilgrims are already going up to Jerusalem for the Jewish feast of the Passover. Among them are also non-Jews who are sympathetic to Judaism, such as the Greeks we are told about today.

Passover was always a time of great tension and expectation, because according to Jewish beliefs the Messiah, the longed-for savior, would reveal himself in Jerusalem at a Passover festival. And many people were wondering, this year, whether the controversial Jesus of Nazareth might not after all be the Messiah.

Jesus did not reject this eager expectation, but he did turn it completely inside out. Yes, the hour had come, he was going to show that he was the Messiah, the Savior—but in a quite different way from what people expected. It was not brilliant success that lay before him, but the hour of his death. Yet his downfall, his apparent failure, would be the real victory he would win.

A simple image from nature shows how fruitfulness can be attained only through total loss: the grain of wheat remains solitary unless it "dies" in the earth so as to bring forth a stalk loaded with ears. Jesus deduced from this a basic principle of human existence: Anyone who is anxiously clinging to and looking after himself will be left on his own and will remain dry and unfruitful. If anyone is willing to risk his life, then that life will be full and blessed.

Yet this attitude arouses fear in us. Letting go is terrifying, and if commitment may require even our lives, then panic sets in. Jesus went through all that in his own life. We already sense here, several days before the drama of the crucifixion, that Jesus is inwardly "shaken" in the core of his being. He must have been tempted to flee. But Jesus knew that God, his Father, had allotted him the task—not of fleeing, but of giving his life. Just as at his baptism in the Jordan, so now, too, a voice from heaven confirmed that exactly this was God's plan for saving us. Jesus had to die, exactly like the little grain of wheat, so as to bring forth many, many grains.

What was difficult to understand at that time is still so to this day: Why should there be suffering, the Cross, and death? Yet why should things be completely different for us from the way they are in nature, where there is no new life without death? And that would certainly be the case for Jesus. His dying on the Cross was going to bring life to many people. Now, looking at the Cross, we too will be able to agree to let go and finally, indeed, to assent to our own death, for it is the gate to new life.

PALM SUNDAY

The Gospel of Mark 11:1–10

[*The Passover of the Jews was near.*] *And when they drew near to Jerusalem, to Bethphage and Bethany, at the Mount of Olives,* [*Jesus*] *sent two of his disciples, and said to them, "Go into the village opposite you, and immediately as you enter it you will find a colt tied, on which no one has ever sat; untie it and bring it. If any one says to you, 'Why are you doing this?' say, 'The Lord has need of it and will send it back here immediately.'" And they went away, and found a colt tied at the door out in the open street; and they untied it. And those who stood there said to them, "What are you doing, untying the colt?" And they told them what Jesus had said; and they let them go. And they brought the colt to Jesus, and threw their garments on it; and he sat upon it. And many spread their garments on the road, and others spread leafy branches which they had cut from the fields. And those who went before and those who followed cried out, "Hosanna! Blessed is he who comes in the name of the Lord! Blessed is the kingdom of our father David that is coming! Hosanna in the highest!"*

❧

The King of Peace Is Coming!

Pilgrims are familiar with it: the joy at seeing for the first time the longed-for goal of the path that has often been long and arduous. At Santiago de Compostela, that place is called Mount Joy (Monte Gozo). Anyone who has come hundreds of miles on pilgrimage feels this joy with particular intensity. Even after only three or four days' walking to Mariazell, we feel it the moment the towers of the basilica come into view.

People on pilgrimage to Jerusalem felt this when they reached the Mount of Olives and suddenly saw Jerusalem before them, especially the beautiful temple, on the spot where the Dome of the Rock stands today. From childhood onward, Jesus had often passed that way and had stopped there a moment with the other pilgrims and sung psalms of joy.

This time it is different. Jesus himself sets the scene for his entry into Jerusalem according to an exact scenario. He has a young donkey fetched for himself. It is astounding—but his disciples have seen and heard so many astounding things with him—that he knows exactly where they can find the donkey he is going to borrow and that everything happens in the way he predicts. It will be just the same, a few days later, when he is taken prisoner, condemned, beaten, and crucified. That, too, he has predicted quite precisely a number of times—and also that that will not be the end; that after three days, he will rise from the dead.

Why on a donkey? Why not on foot, like all the other times? Why not "on a high horse", as only the rich people and the Romans could afford to do? This was a clear sign: in one of the prophets was the following oracle: "Rejoice greatly, O daughter of Zion! . . . Behold, your king comes to you; triumphant and victorious is he, humble and riding on a donkey . . . and he shall command peace to the nations; his dominion shall be from sea to sea" (Zech 9:9–10). The long-expected and yearned-for King of Peace, the Messiah, will (as the prophet sees it) put an end to war and will restore the kingdom of David.

Jesus is declaring quite simply and straightforwardly that he is the one for whom the people have longed. He enters his royal city of Jerusalem, not with military might, but riding on a donkey. So we can understand why the people are rejoicing. All hopes are pinned on him. Thus, we can also understand the disappointment that is soon spreading. For Jesus has come to set up, not a new political kingdom, but the kingdom of God. For many people, their disappointment will soon be changing to fury. On Good Friday they will be yelling, "Crucify him!"

Jesus has not come to make people do things, to over-power them. He is looking, not for political power, but to win people's hearts. He makes his entry into Jerusalem hum-bly, and that is the way he seeks to come to us, to this day. We often wonder why God allows all kinds of things to hap-pen—war and illness and so much suffering. After all, he is almighty; he has the power to intervene and put things straight. He has chosen to show his power in another way, however, and we do not find it easy to assent to this: he wants to make us whole from the roots up, through our turning to God and turning away from evil; through the power of love. That is his peace plan—the only one that really works. Jesus executes it on the Cross. It is for this that he is entering Jerusalem. And that is reason for rejoicing to this day.

The Passion in the Gospel of John 19:17–30

So they took Jesus, and he went out, bearing his own cross, to the place called the place of a skull, which is called in Hebrew Golgotha. There they crucified him, and with him two others, one on either side, and Jesus between them. Pilate also wrote a title and put it on the cross; it read, "Jesus of Nazareth, the King of the Jews." Many of the Jews read this title, for the place where Jesus was crucified was near the city; and it was written in Hebrew, in Latin, and in Greek. The chief priests of the Jews then said to Pilate, "Do not write, 'The King of the Jews,' but, 'This man said, I am King of the Jews.'" Pilate answered, "What I have written I have written."

When the soldiers had crucified Jesus they took his garments and made four parts, one for each soldier; also his tunic. But the tunic was without seam, woven from top to bottom; so they said to one another, "Let us not tear it, but cast lots for it to see whose it shall be." This was to fulfil the Scripture,

"They parted my garments among them,
and for my clothing they cast lots."

So the soldiers did this. But standing by the cross of Jesus were his mother, and his mother's sister, Mary the wife of Clopas, and Mary Magdalene. When Jesus saw his mother, and the disciple whom he loved standing near, he said to his mother, "Woman, behold, your son!" Then he said to the disciple, "Behold, your mother!" And from that hour the disciple took her to his own home.

After this Jesus, knowing that all was now finished, said (to fulfil the Scripture), "I thirst." A bowl full of vinegar stood there; so they put a sponge full of the vinegar on hyssop and held it to his mouth. When Jesus had received the vinegar, he said, "It is finished"; and he bowed his head and gave up his spirit.

༝

A Gaze like No Other

"There they crucified him." Without any ornamentation and without a single word describing the horrors of what happened, John simply records the fact: they crucified him.

How can the heart of man conceive such a horror?

In those days, thousands of people were executed by crucifixion all over the Roman Empire: slaves, criminals, and rebels—and one of them was that Jesus of Nazareth who said that he was King of the Jews.

What happens to someone's heart to make him capable of torturing to death other people who feel pain in precisely the same way as I do myself? How this form of death was carried out can be read, in detail, on that mysterious sheet of cloth that is preserved in Turin. The traces of the scourging, the wounds of the nails, blood around the head, probably from a crown of thorns, a swollen and battered face, and lastly a broad stream of blood from a deep wound in the rib cage.

Scientists have not yet been able to explain the origin of the image of a crucified man on the Turin shroud, but it is shattering evidence of the torment and mortal agony that underlies the brief phrase, "They crucified him."

John, who wrote that, was an eyewitness. The other

174

apostles had all fled, in panic and terror. He, "the disciple whom Jesus loved" (as he called himself, Jn 19:26, 20:2), had stayed with Jesus. He did not need to tell his contemporaries anything about the torments of crucifixion. They all knew well enough. He could concentrate entirely on what distinguished this man being crucified from all the others.

The notice above the crucified man said who he really was: the King of the Jews, the Promised One, the Messiah, the Redeemer and Savior of his people. Pilate insisted on writing that. Was he intending to annoy Jesus' Jewish accusers by doing that, or was he inwardly preoccupied with the question whether Jesus really was who he said he was? Some old legends say that Pilate spent the rest of his life being bothered by that question. To the end of his life, we are told, the accused man whom he had condemned to death—even though he knew in his heart that he was innocent—was standing before his eyes. He could never forget what he said, the way he kept silent, or above all the way he looked at him, that gaze with no trace of condemnation or contempt, which nonetheless penetrated to his inmost soul, the gaze that knew him through and through—the gaze of Jesus!

That gaze had also fallen on John and on Jesus' mother, who was enduring the indescribable pain of seeing her son nailed to the Cross and suffering the throes of death. Jesus provided for them both: his mother was to take his beloved John as her son, and John was to take her for his mother. And that was how it was, from that moment on, as if this was the last will of Jesus.

We can say that Jesus gazed upon his mother, in the literal as in the figurative sense. He provided for her, and at the same time he entrusted her with the task of looking out for his favorite disciple. She took that literally, and since then she has looked out for all those children of men for whom her Son took upon himself that agonizing death. And as Jesus died for all men, since then she has looked out for all men. It is good to know that.

EASTER SUNDAY

———

The Gospel of John 20:1–18

Now on the first day of the week Mary Magdalene came to the tomb early, while it was still dark, and saw that the stone had been taken away from the tomb. So she ran, and went to Simon Peter and the other disciple, the one whom Jesus loved, and said to them, "They have taken the Lord out of the tomb, and we do not know where they have laid him." Peter then came out with the other disciple, and they went toward the tomb. They both ran, but the other disciple outran Peter and reached the tomb first; and stooping to look in, he saw the linen cloths lying there, but he did not go in. Then Simon Peter came, following him, and went into the tomb; he saw the linen cloths lying, and the napkin, which had been on his head, not lying with the linen cloths but rolled up in a place by itself. Then the other disciple, who reached the tomb first, also went in, and he saw and believed; for as yet they did not know the Scripture, that he must rise from the dead. Then the disciples went back to their homes.

But Mary stood weeping outside the tomb, and as she wept she stooped to look into the tomb; and she saw two angels in white, sitting where the body of Jesus had lain, one at the head and one at the feet. They said to her, "Woman, why are you weeping?" She said to them, "Because they have taken away my Lord, and I do not know where they have laid him." Saying this, she turned round and saw Jesus standing, but she did not know that it was Jesus. Jesus said to her, "Woman, why are you weeping?

Whom do you seek?" Supposing him to be the gardener, she said to him, "Sir, if you have carried him away, tell me where you have laid him, and I will take him away." Jesus said to her, "Mary." She turned and said to him in Hebrew, "Rabboni!" (which means Teacher). Jesus said to her, "Do not hold me, for I have not yet ascended to the Father; but go to my brethren and say to them, I am ascending to my Father and your Father, to my God and your God." Mary Magdalene went and said to the disciples, "I have seen the Lord"; and she told them that he had said these things to her.

৯৯

Woman, Why Are You Weeping?

Where were those gentlemen, the apostles? All of them, with just one exception, had run away, had abandoned their Master when he was arrested and condemned and when he was driven forth to crucifixion bearing the beam destined for his agony. Only the youngest of them, John, had stayed with him, along with Mary, the mother of Jesus, and a few women, especially that Mary of Magdala whom he had rescued from her sinful way of life.

They had all gone—hiding somewhere or other, panic-stricken and terrified. And if a certain Joseph of Arimathea had not taken care of his body, the apostles would have left Jesus hanging on the Cross, and he would finally have ended up in a mass grave, like the others who were crucified.

The women had stood up to it far better: first his mother, who stood by him in the hour of his death agony. Nor did the other women from Galilee allow themselves to be deprived of human sympathy by their fear. Among them, the one from Magdala stands out particularly.

She was already at the grave, before sunrise. She was struck with fear. The heavy stone had been rolled away, and the tomb stood empty. She ran to the apostles, and two of them hurried back, saw the same thing—and went away again, still at a loss.

Yet she stayed. She wept. She could not come to terms with this; she was looking for him. Love does not give up or run away. She stayed. And thus she was the first person to see Jesus, no longer as a dead man, but alive.

Easter morning is the most important day in history. For that night, Christ rose from the dead. From Easter morning onward, the ineluctable law of death was overruled, and death was no longer final. No longer would death have the last word.

Yet this, the most lovely of all mornings, did not begin with any fanfare. There were no mass media there, no crowds —just a weeping woman. And as the first utterance of the new age, the mighty conqueror of death put only a simple question, expressing human sympathy: "Woman, why are you weeping?" His first concern, after the Resurrection, was to comfort someone. The time will come when God shall wipe away every tear. That time began on Easter morning.

"Mary!" he said to her—and then she recognized him: it is he! He is alive! And since that Easter morning, he has called countless people by name, including his fearful apostles, whom he still, in spite of everything, called "My brothers". And I dare to say it: me, too. I know that he is alive, that he dries my tears as well.

Since then, he has sent countless people out to pass on this joyful news. I, too, can come to you today with this Easter greeting.

SECOND SUNDAY OF EASTER
(DIVINE MERCY SUNDAY)

———

The Gospel of John 20:19–31

On the evening of that day, the first day of the week, the doors being shut where the disciples were, for fear of the Jews, Jesus came and stood among them and said to them, "Peace be with you." When he had said this, he showed them his hands and his side. Then the disciples were glad when they saw the Lord. Jesus said to them again, "Peace be with you. As the Father has sent me, even so I send you." And when he had said this, he breathed on them, and said to them, "Receive the Holy Spirit. If you forgive the sins of any, they are forgiven; if you retain the sins of any, they are retained."

Now Thomas, one of the Twelve, called the Twin, was not with them when Jesus came. So the other disciples told him, "We have seen the Lord." But he said to them, "Unless I see in his hands the print of the nails, and place my finger in the mark of the nails, and place my hand in his side, I will not believe."

Eight days later, his disciples were again in the house, and Thomas was with them. The doors were shut, but Jesus came and stood among them, and said, "Peace be with you." Then he said to Thomas, "Put your finger here, and see my hands; and put out your hand, and place it in my side; do not be faithless, but believing." Thomas answered him, "My Lord and my God!" Jesus said to him, "You have believed because you have seen me. Blessed are those who have not seen and yet believe."

Now Jesus did many other signs in the presence of the disciples, which are not written in this book; but these are written that you may believe that Jesus is the Christ, the Son of God, and that believing you may have life in his name.

Immeasurably Merciful

Łagiewniki is a suburb of Krakow. There, in 1938, a simple religious sister died; Faustina Kowalska was her name in religion. She was only thirty-three years old and not particularly educated, with undistinguished responsibilities in the convent.

Yet she did have "mystical graces", a special relationship with Christ, and received "speeches", messages from heaven that she had to pass on. At their heart was the message that God's mercy is unfathomable and unlimited. This was to be declared to all men and taught to tormented mankind.

Pope John Paul II said in Łagiewniki, in the big new church there, that he wanted this message to reach all mankind. In 2000, in Rome, he had declared Sister Faustina a saint.

Why do I mention this today, in particular? Because Sister Faustina time and again received a command from heaven to say that the Sunday after Easter Day, the so-called Low Sunday (White Sunday in some countries), should be celebrated as the Feast of Mercy. And indeed the Holy Father did celebrate the "Low Sunday" of the great Jubilee Year, in 2000, as "Divine Mercy Sunday" for the first time.

What has all that got to do with doubting Thomas, who was prepared to believe only what he could "grasp" with his eyes and his hands? There are many people who sympathize with him, this apostle who is so ready to admit quite openly his difficulties in believing. That is why we ourselves have the confidence to speak about them.

I often wonder whether the most common difficulty of all is that of not believing in God's mercy. "Do not be faithless, but believing", says Jesus to the Apostle Thomas. Believing that God loves me so much that the most precious thing he has is not too good for me—his own Son; believing that God really does not despise me or condemn me because of my having so many faults that I often dislike myself and find myself unbearable; believing that God's mercy is greater than all our failures—that is what Jesus was trying to say to all men through Sister Faustina. That is his good news. It brings that peace which Jesus wished to his disciples on the evening of Easter Day. That is what Jesus, the Risen One, wants from his apostles: for them to bring the peace of his mercy to everyone, to all peoples. And to that end, he brought them the loveliest Easter present: "If you forgive the sins of any, they are forgiven."

What do we have to do? "Blessed are those who have not seen, and yet believe." Happy is anyone who trusts in Jesus completely, who finds his refuge in his mercy. It is inexhaustible!

The Gospel of Luke 24:35–48

[*The two disciples who had returned from Emmaus*] *told what had happened on the road, and how* [*Jesus*] *was known to them in the breaking of the bread.*

As they were saying this, Jesus himself stood among them, and said to them, "Peace to you." But they were startled and frightened, and supposed that they saw a spirit. And he said to them, "Why are you troubled, and why do questionings rise in your hearts? See my hands and my feet, that it is I myself; handle me, and see; for a spirit has not flesh and bones as you see that I have." And when he had said this he showed them his hands and his feet. And while they still disbelieved for joy, and wondered, he said to them, "Have you anything here to eat?" They gave him a piece of broiled fish, and he took it and ate before them.

Then he said to them, "These are my words which I spoke to you, while I was still with you, that everything written about me in the law of Moses and the prophets and the psalms must be fulfilled." Then he opened their minds to understand the Scriptures, and said to them, "Thus it is written, that the Christ should suffer and on the third day rise from the dead, and that repentance and forgiveness of sins should be preached in his name to all nations, beginning from Jerusalem. You are witnesses of these things."

ﻊ

Subject Number One: Resurrection

For fifty days, from Easter to Pentecost, Sunday by Sunday, there is just one great subject, one theme: the Resurrection of Jesus; and then it continues, Sunday by Sunday, throughout the whole year: once more, this one theme: the Resurrection of Jesus.

Every Sunday is, so to speak, a celebration of Easter. What made Sunday into Sunday was this once-for-all event of Jesus rising from the dead. That distinguishes this day from all the other days of the week.

The way Christians understand it, Sunday is not the "weekend", but the first day of the week. For a new era, a new life, starts with the Resurrection.

But are we still aware of that today? Why is the Resurrection the number-one subject of the Christian faith? And why did this subject, right from the start, meet with so much misunderstanding and contradiction, with mockery and rejection? What was the reason for it? Today's Gospel reading mentions quite specifically the two main difficulties with belief in the Resurrection.

When, on the evening of the day of his Resurrection from the tomb, this first of all Sundays, Jesus suddenly appeared in the midst of his apostles, their spontaneous reaction was not one of peace and joy; it was that of fear and horror. They could not comprehend it; they were in doubt, and only powerful evidence such as being able to touch his body, watching while he ate something before their eyes, would allow joy to well up within them.

The first difficulty, which still persists, is this: Why a bodily resurrection? Do we not survive beyond death in any case (in some way or other)? Why should we be given a body again—

and if we are, then what kind of body can it be? It is not surprising that so many people who entirely accept the idea of life beyond death cannot see the point of the resurrection of the body.

Yet it was precisely this to which the apostles are said to have witnessed at the time, and all Christians since then. Jesus' wish was that this good news be carried to all peoples.

The news of Jesus' Resurrection is joyful, however, only in connection with the second difficulty. This was, and still is, the greatest stumbling block. It is the fact that before Jesus rose from the dead, he died on the Cross; before Easter comes Good Friday. The fact that their Master had died that terrible death on the Cross appeared to the apostles to be a sheer, meaningless horror. That was the collapse of all their hopes, their absolute disappointment. And then Jesus came along and patiently showed them how it all had to be that way, that this was God's plan, and not merely human cruelty.

The Cross was no accident; it was not an unfortunate working of chance; it was the way God himself had chosen in order to grant as a gift to all men freedom from the burden of their sins.

On Easter morning Jesus rose from the grave. God confirmed that his death on the Cross was no meaningless annihilation. His suffering was not in vain. Yet in that case, my suffering, too, is not in vain. If his Cross was the path to his new life, then my cross, too, may be for me the passage to my resurrection. Jesus, open my eyes, that I may understand!

The Gospel of John 10:11–18

[Jesus said,] "I am the good shepherd. The good shepherd lays down his life for the sheep. He who is a hireling and not a shepherd, whose own the sheep are not, sees the wolf coming and leaves the sheep and flees; and the wolf snatches them and scatters them. He flees because he is a hireling and cares nothing for the sheep. I am the good shepherd; I know my own and my own know me, as the Father knows me and I know the Father; and I lay down my life for the sheep. And I have other sheep, that are not of this fold; I must bring them also, and they will heed my voice. So there shall be one flock, one shepherd. For this reason the Father loves me, because I lay down my life, that I may take it again. No one takes it from me, but I lay it down of my own accord. I have power to lay it down, and I have power to take it again; this charge I have received from my Father."

A Shepherd like No Other

In old photos of my homeland in Bohemia I see our shepherd, with his broad-brimmed hat and his loden coat, leaning against a tree, knitting a woolen sock. Beside him is his sheepdog, and all around the flock of sheep—it is a picture from a bygone age, a world not much different, essentially, from in Jesus' time. Only the wolves Jesus talks about, which used to prey on the flocks, are no longer to be found in our land. They were active for the last time in the cold winters of the twenties.

I know all that only from what old people tell me and from yellowing photos. Has the image of the good shepherd therefore become incomprehensible for us in today's world? I do not think so. I believe that what Jesus says about the good shepherd still stirs people's spirits just as much, even though the shepherd with his flock has become a rare sight. Perhaps this is because the good shepherd who cares for the sheep is a kind of archetypal image in our minds. It is probably also on account of the power of Jesus' own words. It is not the shepherd who makes clear what Jesus is saying, but vice versa: only through Jesus do we feel the full force and depth of the image of the good shepherd. For there is no shepherd like him.

"The good shepherd lays down his life for the sheep." What moves us about this image is the feeling of security we have. His sheep are just as important to this shepherd as his own life—even more important. At the critical moment he does not run away, does not abandon his charges in order to keep himself safe and save his own skin. Anyone with a shepherd like that knows he is safe.

How badly we all need people like that, people who do not think only about themselves and their own comfort. How very much do children need such parents, workers such bosses, and believers such priests and bishops. How very much we need people who undertake their tasks, not merely as a job, but as pastoral care.

The good shepherd does not abandon his flock when "things get hot", when the wolf becomes a threat to the flock. Part of a pastor's task is being prepared to stand up in person to evil, to what may hurt people—not to let things run their course so as to avoid taking unpleasant steps.

Parents are good shepherds whenever they do not simply let everything pass, when they protect their children from negative influences. And Christ, the "chief shepherd", expects the shepherds of the Church, the pastors, to have the courage not just to say "yes" and "Amen" to everything, merely to avoid rubbing people the wrong way. Jesus set an example of how the shepherd has to protect those who belong to him, even at the cost of being unpopular.

"I know my own and my own know me." The shepherd knows his flock, and his flock knows him. We usually know pretty quickly whether a "shepherd" is concerned for us or for himself. Children are hurt, not by their parents being strict, but by the feeling that they do not matter to their parents. We are deeply moved when we meet people who are good shepherds. And God be thanked, they are there: in the family, in professional life, in politics, and in the Church. They impart what we need so much, a feeling of care and security. We should be grateful to them. Yet no one is more of a shepherd, in that sense, than Jesus himself. No one loves us as he does. Only he is wholly and completely "the good shepherd".

The Gospel of John 15:1–8

[Jesus said to his disciples,] "I am the true vine, and my Father is the vinedresser. Every branch of mine that bears no fruit, he takes away, and every branch that does bear fruit he prunes, that it may bear more fruit. You are already made clean by the word which I have spoken to you. Abide in me, and I in you. As the branch cannot bear fruit by itself, unless it abides in the vine, neither can you, unless you abide in me. I am the vine, you are the branches. He who abides in me, and I in him, he it is that bears much fruit, for apart from me you can do nothing. If a man does not abide in me, he is cast forth as a branch and withers; and the branches are gathered, thrown into the fire and burned. If you abide in me, and my words abide in you, ask whatever you will, and it shall be done for you. By this my Father is glorified, that you bear much fruit, and so prove to be my disciples."

ॐ

The True Vine

For people who live where I, as a wine drinker, would like to live, in Retz (Lower Austria), today's Gospel reading is easy to understand and quite concrete. Who among them does not know what work the vinedresser does when he has to trim back or cut away many branches so that the vine may bear good fruit? Who is not familiar with the picture of the vine branches that have been cut off and are then collected and burned? In the old days, people used to tie them in bundles and cut them up to use as fuel for fires and stoves. Everyone knows that as soon as a vine branch is cut off, it withers. Jesus could not possibly express it more graphically: Once separated from me, the true vine, you can no more produce anything than can a rotting branch in the vineyard. Hence, the main point: "Remain in me, and I remain in you!"

I think that what Jesus meant was this: If the life-giving sap is not flowing from the vine into the branches, then no fruit will grow. If we do not have a real, living contact with God, with Jesus his Son, then we are quite as dead as vine branches lying on the ground.

We are dead without God. For God is the life of our life. And since he is the God of life, he does not wish for us to die; rather, he wishes that we should live. And here again, the image of viticulture helps us to see how God brings us alive.

Anyone seeing how the vinedresser prunes the vine in winter, cutting all the branches right back, might have the impression—if he knows nothing about it himself—that nothing more could come from the stump of the vine. The opposite is true. Only thus can it shoot forth strongly again in the spring.

In the Bible, the vineyard is often an image for the people of God. Sometimes it seems cut back so much that many people declare it to be already dead. Yet it then shoots forth again, a new and living growth. That is what we can see in history, right up to this day. Often said to be dead, the Church experiences a "new spring" time and again.

But the vinedresser also trims the vines back. That is his work in spring and summer. The branches must not shoot out too vigorously, otherwise the fruit will not grow properly. God is the vinedresser for our lives. Many of the cuts hurt—tribulations of all kinds that God allows to come on us to cleanse us. Experience teaches us that we can grow and stay alive only if God works on us as the good vinedresser. He knows what are unfruitful shoots for us and what has to be got rid of. He knows us through and through, and he tries to set us free from wrong inclinations and from self-deception.

Jesus is the true vine, in whom the life-giving sap of God is flowing. Nothing works without him—that is what he tells us unequivocally. We may indeed be doing a lot and be very active; but without Christ, nothing will come of it: "Abide in me!"

It is not the person who utters many words who is abiding in Christ but the one who loves his neighbor. That is the fruit that God expects from us, the only really good fruit. For without love, we are nothing but dead branches.

The Gospel of John 15:9–17

[Jesus said to his disciples,] "As the Father has loved me, so have I loved you; abide in my love. If you keep my commandments, you will abide in my love, just as I have kept my Father's commandments and abide in his love. These things I have spoken to you, that my joy may be in you, and that your joy may be full.

"This is my commandment, that you love one another as I have loved you. Greater love has no man than this, that a man lay down his life for his friends. You are my friends if you do what I command you. No longer do I call you servants, for the servant does not know what his master is doing; but I have called you friends, for all that I have heard from my Father I have made known to you. You did not choose me, but I chose you and appointed you that you should go and bear fruit and that your fruit should abide; so that whatever you ask the Father in my name, he may give it to you. This I command you, to love one another."

ই

A Friend in Spite of It All

Nothing does you more good than to know you are loved. No material wealth, no matter what good health, can equal being loved. It corresponds to our deepest human need, to be accepted, to feel that I am important for someone, am affirmed and wanted.

There is no sun beneath which we bloom more beautifully than the sun of love. And when it no longer shines on us, we shrink like plants without sunshine.

Jesus is talking about this in today's Gospel reading. He does so just a few hours before his arrest and his execution on the Cross. He knows that in a short time almost everyone will abandon him, and nonetheless he calls them "friends" right now. We expect friends to be loyal, especially in need. Experience does show, of course, that it is then, when the going is tough and things go wrong, that friends are few. Then it becomes clear who our real friends are. The apostles did not show themselves friends to Jesus. In fear for their own lives, they abandoned him.

Yet he stayed loyal to them. He was truly the good friend, in spite of their cowardice. They were most deeply moved that Jesus forgave them for betraying him, that he did not say they were no longer his friends, as we usually do if friends leave us when we are in need. It must have been incomprehensible to them that he made no reproach, did not call them to account for their mistakes, appeared to them on Easter Day.

When we find in practice a friend who is disloyal and betrays us, we usually demand an explanation from him, something to "make up for what has happened", an explanation of his wrong behavior, and apologies. Only then are we (maybe) ready to resume our friendship. Jesus behaved differently. He did not simply forgive his friends their betrayal in advance, but he did something that only the best and most loyal of friends would do: he gave up his life for his friends.

We quite rightly admire people who risk their lives to save others. We owe them gratitude and recognition. I think for instance of my aunt, who after the war obtained the medicine that saved me at the risk of her life.

Jesus did not shrink even from death on the Cross in order to save us. That is what he is talking about in today's Gospel reading. He mentions his reason for acting thus: "That is how I have loved you."

He asks nothing by way of equivalent response from us; he expects only that we love one another as he has loved us. And he promises us, "If you remain in this love, then you will know great joy; and then your life will not run its course without results; and then you will bring other people to blossom, as well; then people will be happy to be with you and alongside you."

Basically it is so simple—just as simple as the way Jesus talks about it: "Love one another!" And yet we know that it is not at all easy to love when there is no love returned; to forgive when we meet with ingratitude. That is exactly what Jesus met with from his friends, and he has offered us an example of what it is like when someone remains a friend in spite of it all—a real friend.

———

The Gospel of Mark 16:15–20

[Jesus appeared to the Eleven] and he said to them, "Go into all the world and preach the gospel to the whole creation. He who believes and is baptized will be saved; but he who does not believe will be condemned. And these signs will accompany those who believe: in my name they will cast out demons; they will speak in new tongues; they will pick up serpents, and if they drink any deadly thing, it will not hurt them; they will lay their hands on the sick, and they will recover."

So then the Lord Jesus, after he had spoken to them, was taken up into heaven, and sat down at the right hand of God. And they went forth and preached everywhere, while the Lord worked with them and confirmed the message by the signs that attended it.

The Sending of the Eleven

That is how it began: a tiny troop of eleven men with a worldwide task. The contrast could not be greater. How was this team of eleven to go out "into all the world" and bring the good news of Jesus to all creatures? And yet it did come about—not, indeed, at once, not even in the apostles' own lifetime, but in the course of the centuries—so that today, around two billion people all over the world, from among all peoples, languages, and countries, are Christians.

Jesus gave them a worldwide mission. How did he understand this? Certainly not as "making people be happy". His disciples were to "proclaim" the gospel but not compel anyone's assent. They were to make it known but not to make people accept it. Just as the offer has to respect freedom, so equally the answer must be free.

One thing Jesus did, of course, make clear: His gospel, which the apostles were to take to "all creation", demands a response: assent or rejection, belief or unbelief. And at that point, Jesus became "unsociably" sharp: Anyone who accepts what is offered "will be saved"; anyone who rejects it "will be condemned". So there is no free choice, after all? What kind of freedom is it, when I am told, "You can choose for yourself, but if you refuse my offer, you will perish miserably?" That is the same as, "Look out, if you don't do what I say!"

That is not quite so absurd as it might seem at first glance. Of course I am free to choose which way I go. Yet I know that many paths lead to misfortune, and to take one of those means I am misusing my freedom. If I take the path of a mania for gambling, that of alcohol or of drugs, I am free to do so—to start with, at least. After that, it becomes increasingly a path of torment and despair.

It is the same if I choose the path of sin. Jesus, however, offers us a way out, a genuine new start. Jesus gave to the Eleven the task of making this way known throughout the world, the way that leads from death to life, from misfortune to happiness. Anyone is free to venture onto that path or not. Yet because Jesus is God, and not a man with merely human limitations, he knows with divine certainty which is the path that brings happiness. Believing him means trusting him to know the way. Believing him means trusting that his path is the right one, which we would not be able to find on our own.

Yet Jesus does not expect a blind faith. He points to clear signs that confirm the fact that the way of his good news is the right one, the suitable one for man. Anyone who puts his trust in him and believes him will be able to cope with the most difficult situations. Thus, he will be able to survive the poison of hatred; will be unscathed by the snakebites of jealousy, envy, and pride; will not despair in sickness; and will triumph over the snares of the devil. Above all, however, those who believe the gospel will overcome the barriers that so often divide us; for they will talk the language that all people understand, the language of love. And what is more urgent than that the gospel of love, of reconciliation and mercy, should really reach everyone? The task entrusted to the Eleven must be carried forward!

The Gospel of John 17:6a, 11b–19

[*Jesus lifted up his eyes to heaven and said, "Father,*] *I have manifested your name to the men whom you gave me out of the world. . . . Holy Father, keep them in your name, which you have given me, that they may be one, even as we are one. While I was with them, I kept them in your name, which you have given me; I have guarded them, and none of them is lost but the son of perdition, that the Scripture might be fulfilled. But now I am coming to you; and these things I speak in the world, that they may have my joy fulfilled in themselves. I have given them your word; and the world has hated them because they are not of the world, even as I am not of the world. I do not pray that you should take them out of the world, but that you should keep them from the evil one. They are not of the world, even as I am not of the world. Sanctify them in the truth; your word is truth. As you sent me into the world, so I have sent them into the world. And for their sake I consecrate myself, that they also may be consecrated in truth."*

❧

The Testament of Jesus

Jesus is praying out loud. It is the last hour before his Passion and his Cross. Within the trusted circle of his disciples, he opens his heart to them as never before. He is praying before them, a quite personal prayer, expressing his most intimate concerns, his most fervent petitions to God his Father.

This prayer is like his last will and testament. In contrast to our wills, Jesus' words are not directed to controlling what should happen to his property after his death (indeed, he has no earthly property at all). The "provisions of his will" are requests to God. He puts everything into the hands of his Father in heaven; he confides to his care all those he loves. What is Jesus' "last will"?

What a mother who is going to die asks for her children: that God may keep them from the Evil One and that they may remain at one with one another. In the face of death, the parents' first care is not for their children's careers, but that they should not wander from the straight and narrow and should not quarrel among themselves.

Up to now, Jesus has been able to look after his disciples himself, keep them on the right track, and protect them from all evil. Now, however, the hour has come for him to go back to his Father. And just as Jesus has hitherto put complete trust in God, his Father, even more so now, when he is having to let go of it all.

It is a good idea to read this prayer out loud, as Jesus spoke it out loud in front of the others. It rouses, in anyone who hears it, the longing to be able likewise to pray so trustingly, so earnestly. It made an unforgettable impression on the apostles, being able to see Jesus praying time and again, and now, at the Last Supper, to hear him as well. What must it have been like when Jesus said "Father!" like that? Here, praying is not about a vague feeling of there being some higher power; rather, it is about an intimate relationship with someone addressed directly and familiarly. "You, Father"— this form of address assumes the most intimate sharing. And what Jesus is asking of this "you", above all else, is that we, too, should come to have an approach to God just as trusting as his own; that we should know something of the joy that springs from being at one with God in this way.

That is why Jesus asks that we may be protected from all evil that might damage or destroy this oneness. He does not ask that we should encounter no difficulties, no trials or suffering, but that we may be kept safe from all evil. As long as we are in this world, there will be struggles, suffering, and danger. What Jesus asks is that with God's help we may come through all these without falling into the hands of the Evil One, without being corrupted by him.

And yet Jesus does more. He does not pray merely for those who belong to him, he also "sacrifices" his life for them. That is what the words "for their sake I consecrate myself" mean, in Jewish usage. We sometimes come across parents who quite consciously offer their life or their death "as a sacrifice" for their children, who accept what hurts them as a sacrifice for the well-being and the salvation of their children and endure it as such. For many people that may be hard to understand; it may seem pointless. Such an offering, however, is certainly what Jesus understood his suffering to be. "For you"—for all men—I give up my life: that was, and remains, his last will and testament. Jesus himself explains it thus, "Greater love has no man than this, that a man lay down his life for his friends."

PENTECOST

———

The Gospel of John 20:19–23

On the evening of that day, the first day of the week, the doors being shut where the disciples were, for fear of the Jews, Jesus came and stood among them and said to them, "Peace be with you." When he had said this, he showed them his hands and his side. Then the disciples were glad when they saw the Lord. Jesus said to them again, "Peace be with you. As the Father has sent me, even so I send you." And when he had said this, he breathed on them, and said to them, "Receive the Holy Spirit. If you forgive the sins of any, they are forgiven; if you retain the sins of any, they are retained."

❧

Shalom!

To this day, "Shalom!" is the most common everyday greeting in Israel. The risen Jesus greets his friends twice, straight off, with this expression: "Peace be with you!"

Wishing each other peace is a lovely custom, which is that much more easily understood, and makes better sense, when it is done in a world full of hatred, terror, and the absence of peace. It expresses a deep longing for peace, which is of course constantly struggling against new setbacks and disappointments. Today, fifty days after Easter, on the Feast of Pentecost, with which the season of Easter ends, we hear once more about the risen Christ's first meeting with his disciples.

In this brief account, I see a strong and substantial response to our longing for peace. How and in what sense does Jesus bring peace with him, so that the Apostle Paul will say, later, that Christ himself is our peace (cf. Eph 2:14)?

We find a miserable handful of fearful, dejected disciples of Jesus. They have barricaded themselves (probably in the room where the Last Supper was held) behind barred doors, on account of a justifiable fear that someone might come and arrest them for being among the friends of the man who was crucified.

Suddenly, Jesus was there. No walls, no doors, no locks or bolts offer any obstacle to him. Maybe they were terrified for a moment, when he was suddenly standing in their midst. Yet his greeting, "Shalom!" immediately brought them what he was saying: peace, and straight after that, an indescribable joy.

People have continued to find this ever since Easter: the presence of Jesus means peace and joy. How does that come about? I believe the Gospel gives us a clue. First of all, Jesus shows them "his hands and his side", that is, the traces of his wounds: the wounds of the nails in his hands, that of the spear deep in his side, right to his heart. Jesus is alive, but the wounds are still visible, not as scars, but as if luminescent, transfigured.

Often in life, when someone has passed through a great sorrow, there comes a profound peace. The wounds are there, but they no longer hurt; rather, they are shining like something precious. Anyone who has undergone such an experience and has matured and grown as a result will look back on such difficult moments with gratitude. They offer an intimation of the resurrection.

Jesus makes no reproach to the apostles: "Why did you

abandon me? Why did you run away like cowards?" Jesus brings peace by not pinning us down to our failures, by granting us the chance to start again. How many situations there are in which peace is possible only if a new start is truly made!

At Easter, however, what Jesus brings makes such a new start possible: the Holy Spirit and the forgiveness of sins. The Holy Spirit, whom Jesus vouchsafed to the apostles at Easter and to the whole Church at Pentecost, is the power behind all new starts. He makes courageous witnesses out of the fearful disciples; and out of a scared Church, shielding herself from the world, he makes a lively and open community. That is how the spirit of Jesus works to this day, always surprising us with something new.

But above all there is peace wherever guilt is pardoned, when sins are forgiven. Because Jesus brought this gift with him on Easter Day, he is the one who truly brings peace. Wherever God's forgiveness is brought to bear among men, that is when the everyday greeting becomes a living reality: Shalom!

FEASTS

IN THE CHURCH YEAR

TRINITY SUNDAY

The Gospel of Matthew 28:16–20

*Now the eleven disciples went to Galilee, to the mountain
to which Jesus had directed them. And when they saw him
they worshiped him; but some doubted. And Jesus came
and said to them, "All authority in heaven and on earth
has been given to me. Go therefore and make disciples of all
nations, baptizing them in the name of the Father and of
the Son and of the Holy Spirit, teaching them to observe all
that I have commanded you; and behold, I am with you
always, to the close of the age."*

Three in One

The Sunday after Pentecost is known as Trinity Sunday. In
many places, you can see representations of the Trinity. I will
just instance the splendid Plague Pillar or Trinity Pillar on the
ramparts of Vienna, the picture at the pilgrim shrine on
Sonntagberg in Lower Austria, and the many pictures of the
throne of mercy at the roadside or in the fields, in wayside
shrines or chapels.

God the Father is usually shown as being elderly, with a
long beard; God the Son, on the Cross, which is being held
by God the Father; and the Holy Spirit as a dove, between
the two of them. Many people raise a critical question: Can
we, should we try to represent God visually at all? Judaism
and Islam explicitly forbid it. A "picture of God" would be

unthinkable in a mosque, even more so a picture of God as Trinity. "You worship three gods" is a common criticism of Christianity.

Today's Gospel reading provides an answer to that accusation. It is the last five verses of the Gospel of Matthew, its solemn conclusion. Some powerful things are said about Jesus here. First, the fact that the man who died on the Cross is alive. He was not just apparently dead; he did really die, as was confirmed by his being pierced to the heart by the soldier's spear. They really did bury him. On the third day, he genuinely rose from the dead, not revived for a further earthly life of limited duration, but having passed beyond death, in a life that is indestructible.

At the agreed meeting place in his Galilean homeland, the disciples see him. Adoration is mingled with doubt. They cannot comprehend it—and yet it is really true; thus their action in falling down before him: an action that is really appropriate only for God, for it is not permissible to worship a man. Yet the words Jesus says to them are unforgettable. They echo down the centuries. They retain their force so long as mankind pursues its way on earth. They encompass all peoples, all men of all eras; they hold good for the whole universe.

There are only two possibilities: either these words are true, or Jesus was fantasizing wildly, a complete lunatic. Who can say, "All authority in heaven and on earth has been given to me"? Only someone who is God can say something like that. Only God is all-powerful. Only if Jesus is God can he pronounce these words without presumption. Only if Jesus is the Son of God has he the right to urge that all men should become his disciples. If a mortal man were to expect all people on earth to become his followers, he would be immeasurably exaggerating his own importance. God however, who created all things, can invite his creatures to trust him entirely.

Because Jesus is genuinely a man, we can make a picture of him. Because Jesus is genuinely God, he can promise, "I am with you always, forever, through all ages." Because Jesus is both God and man, he can invite all men to become his friends, his disciples.

Christians do not worship three gods. They worship the one God, the Father who of his love has given to men what is most precious to him, his Son, and also his "breath of life", the Holy Spirit. Pictures of the Trinity are trying to express, through the limited means of art, what can be grasped only by faith.

The Gospel of Mark 14:12–26 *

On the first day of Unleavened Bread, when they sacrificed the Passover lamb, his disciples said to him, "Where will you have us go and prepare for you to eat the Passover?" And he sent two of his disciples, and said to them, "Go into the city, and a man carrying a jar of water will meet you; follow him, and wherever he enters, say to the householder, 'The Teacher says, Where is my guest room, where I am to eat the Passover with my disciples?' And he will show you a large upper room furnished and ready; there prepare for us." And the disciples set out and went to the city, and found it as he had told them; and they prepared the Passover.

And when it was evening he came with the Twelve. And as they were at table eating, Jesus said, "Truly, I say to you, one of you will betray me, one who is eating with me." They began to be sorrowful, and to say to him one after another, "Is it I?" He said to them, "It is one of the Twelve, one who is dipping bread in the same dish with me. For the Son of man goes as it is written of him, but woe to that man by whom the Son of man is betrayed! It would have been better for that man if he had not been born."

And as they were eating, he took bread, and blessed, and broke it, and gave it to them, and said, "Take; this is my body." And he took a chalice, and when he had given thanks he gave it to them, and they all drank of it. And he

---

* The Missal abbreviates this reading by omitting verses 17–21.

said to them, "This is my blood of the covenant, which is poured out for many. Truly, I say to you, I shall not drink again of the fruit of the vine until that day when I drink it new in the kingdom of God."

And when they had sung a hymn, they went out to the Mount of Olives.

៛៛

Whose Bread I Eat . . .

An old saying runs, "Whose bread I eat, his tune I sing." That expresses a view of life based on sobering and often bitter experience. "The one who pays gives the order", people say. I have to try to please whoever is "providing my bread". If I am dependent on someone, I have to give way to him, try to get on with him, in brief, "sing his tune".

Today, on the feast of Corpus Christi, I should like to interpret that saying in a positive sense. Today, in many places in our country, with joyful and colorful celebration, we are singing the song of him whose bread we eat in the Holy Eucharist. We go out into the streets, the squares, and the roads of our parishes, with music and often with elaborate costumes, with the canopy of "heaven" in the midst, borne by four "heaven carriers", and beneath it the priest with the monstrance, with the Holy of Holies, Christ in the simple shape of bread. There is much folklore here, but also much profound and genuine piety—and why should the two not go together?

And yet, is it not all miles away from what there was at the beginning, what the Gospel tells us about? What do we know about the origin of it all, and what has remained of that?

Everything began with a special supper, which our Jewish fellow citizens celebrate up to this day: with the Passover meal, probably in the year 30 of our current era.

Thousands of pilgrims were in Jerusalem for the paschal festival, Pesach, the greatest festival of the year, when the Jews celebrated the way they were saved from slavery in Egypt at the exodus.

Jesus, too, was celebrating the Passover meal with his disciples in a specially prepared room on the second floor of a house that the owner had willingly made available to the pilgrims from Galilee.

The meal ran its usual course, following the ancient Jewish ritual. And then something quite astonishing happened. Instead of the customary blessing of the bread, Jesus broke the bread and said, "Take; this is my body." And at the end of the meal he took the cup of wine, and instead of the formula of blessing provided for, he said, "This is my blood of the covenant, which is poured out for many."

These were moments never to be forgotten, for this was their last supper together; straight afterward came the arrest and trial, the death sentence, Cross, and grave—and then the Easter morning of the Resurrection.

Jesus had said to them, "Do this in remembrance of me" (Lk 22:19; 1 Cor 11:24–25). And from those very first days, his disciples did it. Again and again, especially on Sunday, the weekly "little Passover", they came together—and still do— to do what Jesus did on that unforgettable night: "This is my body which is given for you, for all men."

Since then the Church has lived on this bread, which is he himself, who does not cease to give his life to men. Anyone who can accept that in his heart, in faith, will also feel the need to celebrate that occasionally and to sing for him whose bread he eats.

———

The Gospel of Luke 2:22–40

When the time came for their purification according to the law of Moses, [the parents of Jesus] brought him up to Jerusalem to present him to the Lord (as it is written in the law of the Lord, "Every male that opens the womb shall be called holy to the Lord") and to offer a sacrifice according to what is said in the law of the Lord, "a pair of turtledoves, or two young pigeons." Now there was a man in Jerusalem, whose name was Simeon, and this man was righteous and devout, looking for the consolation of Israel, and the Holy Spirit was upon him. And it had been revealed to him by the Holy Spirit that he should not see death before he had seen the Lord's Christ. And inspired by the Spirit he came into the temple; and when the parents brought in the child Jesus, to do for him according to the custom of the law, he took him up in his arms and blessed God and said,

"Lord, now let your servant depart in peace,
according to your word;
for my eyes have seen your salvation
which you have prepared in the presence of all peoples,
a light for revelation to the Gentiles,
and for glory to your people Israel."

And his father and his mother marveled at what was said about him; and Simeon blessed them and said to Mary his mother,

"Behold, this child is set for the fall and rising
of many in Israel,
and for a sign that is spoken against

213

(and a sword will pierce through your own soul also),
that thoughts out of many hearts may be revealed."

*And there was a prophetess, Anna, the daughter of
Phanuel, of the tribe of Asher; she was of a great age,
having lived with her husband seven years from her virgin-
ity, and as a widow till she was eighty-four. She did not
depart from the temple, worshiping with fasting and prayer
night and day. And coming up at that very hour she gave
thanks to God, and spoke of him to all who were looking
for the redemption of Jerusalem.*

*And when they had performed everything according to
the law of the Lord, they returned into Galilee, to their
own city, Nazareth. And the child grew and became
strong, filled with wisdom; and the favor of God was upon
him.*

୧❧

A Festival of Light

The second of February was for a long time a folk festival. It
was called "Candlemas" (*Maria Lichtmess*, in German). Forty
days after giving birth, according to Jewish law, the mother
had to offer a sacrifice for her purification at the temple in
Jerusalem. The Gospel, however, mentions another reason as
well: every firstborn male, in the Old Testament understanding, was God's property. He was symbolically redeemed with
a sacrifice.

"Purification" and "redemption" may perhaps be alien
concepts to us today. Less strange is what the Gospel places
center stage: Mary and Joseph bring the newborn child to
the temple in order to dedicate him to God. He is their child,
and yet not really theirs. He belongs to God and has been

entrusted to their care. They give him back into God's hands, from whom they have received him.

Many parents, when they bring their child for baptism, do so because they feel and know in their hearts something like this: The child is not their "possession", their "property". That is why it is good to entrust the child entirely to God and to look on him as God's gift, and his life as God's business.

The Gospel reading, however, adds something else: Two old people, Simeon and Anna, come to meet the child. They are not simply showing us that every new birth reminds us how we ourselves are growing older, that one generation replaces another, and that the arrival of young people means saying goodbye to older ones . . . This process is not always so joyful as in Simeon's case, for he has been living for this moment and now says with thanksgiving that he will be happy to leave this world, since he has seen this child.

There is a more profound reason for the joy of these two old people: in the child who is brought to the temple they are greeting the "light for revelation to the Gentiles", the One who will bring salvation to all peoples.

Jesus—the Light of the nations! That is what the Church celebrates in this time of winter, when the days are already getting longer and the darkness weighs less heavily upon our souls. Today, candles are being blessed in every church. In many places, a procession of lights is held. Christ, the Light in the darkness of the world: that is what the candles signify; that is what the procession of lights means. The warm light of the candles stands for the greater light that streams from Christ throughout all ages. At this cold season of the year, it helps me to have a candle burning near to me. In our world, it is not only the winter that is cold; it is often the world of work and even our family. Going up to the child Jesus, as Simeon did, taking him in our arms, and thanking God for this light that is shining in my life and giving it warmth: that is and always has been the real meaning of today's festival of light.

EXALTATION OF THE HOLY CROSS

The Gospel of John 3:13–17

[Jesus said to Nicodemus,] "No one has ascended into heaven but he who descended from heaven, the Son of man. And as Moses lifted up the serpent in the wilderness, so must the Son of man be lifted up, that whoever believes in him may have eternal life."

For God so loved the world that he gave his only-begotten Son, that whoever believes in him should not perish but have eternal life. For God sent the Son into the world, not to condemn the world, but that the world might be saved through him.

৵

A Saving Sight

Today's feast is called the Exaltation of the Holy Cross. On September 14 in the year 335, in Jerusalem, following the solemn dedication of the basilica of the Resurrection (usually known as the Church of the Holy Sepulcher today), there was displayed to the people the Cross of Christ—or more exactly, what remained of it. Since then, September 14 has been celebrated as the Feast of the Exaltation of the Holy Cross.

But what is there to celebrate about the fact that a cross, or the remains of a cross, is found and then displayed? What reason is there for rejoicing and celebration if an instrument of torture and execution of the most appalling kind is held up high?

217

Nicodemus, a member of the great council, comes to Jesus secretly, by night (he is afraid of being seen and criticized for this). He, the learned and well-respected man of wisdom, puts to Jesus the questions he really has at heart. Jesus' answers are both puzzling and marvelous.

First, Jesus says to the astounded councilor that he has to be "born anew". Go back into his mother's womb? No, says Jesus, it is not about that kind of birth, but the one "from above". Man has to be born again from God. But what does that mean? And how does it happen?

Only he who comes "from above" can tell us that, he who is at home, so to speak, in the realm of God and has "come down" to us to tell us about it. And what is the news that he has brought down "from above"? It is incredible, incomprehensibly wonderful news: that God so loved the world that he has given up for it what is most precious to him: his Son. The latter has come, not to judge us, but to save us.

Nicodemus must have been amazed by all that: a God who wishes, not to judge people and punish them, but to save them, for love of us and of all men! Being able to see God like that is really like being born again. Being able to believe that God really loves us is quite a feat. Why do we find believing it so difficult?—Because we are afraid of God. Because we are afraid that he is toward us the way we are toward one another: full of judgments and criticism, contemptuous know-it-alls. We can hardly conceive that God is quite different from us; we are always busy painting a picture of God in our own image. How can our image of God be made new, one not filled with fear but trusting in his love?

Jesus gives Nicodemus some advice about this. He reminds him of the story about the snakes in the wilderness, by which many Israelites had been fatally bitten. Then Moses hung up a bronze serpent on a staff. Anyone who looked up at it did not die from the snakebite. Jesus now says: "You must do the same. Whenever the poisonous serpents of hatred, of mistrust, and of enmity bite you and start to poison you, look up to me on the Cross, and that sight will heal you."

The Cross is a dreadful instrument of execution. Yet Jesus accepted it in order to heal us. That is why looking at the Cross does heal us.

DEDICATION OF THE LATERAN BASILICA

The Gospel of John 2:13–22

The Passover of the Jews was at hand, and Jesus went up to Jerusalem. In the temple he found those who were selling oxen and sheep and pigeons, and the money-changers at their business. And making a whip of cords, he drove them all, with the sheep and oxen, out of the temple; and he poured out the coins of the money-changers and overturned their tables. And he told those who sold the pigeons, "Take these things away; you shall not make my Father's house a house of trade." His disciples remembered that it was written, "Zeal for your house will consume me." The Jews then said to him, "What sign have you to show us for doing this?" Jesus answered them, "Destroy this temple, and in three days I will raise it up." The Jews then said, "It has taken forty-six years to build this temple, and will you raise it up in three days?" But he spoke of the temple of his body. When therefore he was raised from the dead, his disciples remembered that he had said this; and they believed the Scripture and the word which Jesus had spoken.

Feast of the Dedication—Universal

The ninth of November is not a very well-known feast to us. Yet the Church assigns great significance to it, nonetheless, so it is celebrated, not only in Rome, but throughout the universal Church.

It is the Feast of the Dedication of the Lateran Basilica in Rome. For the great majority of visitors to Rome, pilgrims and tourists, Saint Peter's, the Sistine Chapel, and the Vatican museum are far more important.

Only a very few know that it is not Saint Peter's but the Lateran Basilica that is the real cathedral church of the pope, who is in the first instance Bishop of Rome. There it is that the pope, like all his predecessors, has his actual episcopal throne in Rome, even though he lives in the Vatican, next door to Saint Peter's, which is, above all, the memorial church on the tomb of the Apostle Peter.

Today, then, is the dedication feast of the cathedral church of Rome. Above its entrance is written, in Latin, "Mother and head of all the churches". Because the Bishop of Rome, as successor to Saint Peter, has first place among all bishops, his church likewise has this position. The dedication feast in Rome is, so to speak, the dedication feast for the worldwide Church.

The Gospel reading for this feast is of course not so bright and joyful as we normally imagine for a dedication feast. This is the dramatic scene in which Jesus drives the merchants and the money-changers out of the temple in "righteous wrath", that is, just the opposite of our dedication feasts, with their market stalls, merry-go-rounds, and refreshment tents.

Is Jesus appearing as a fanatic here, as an over strict zealot? Was he a revolutionary trying out an uprising here, which then miserably failed and ended with an execution, that of crucifixion, which was usual for sedition in those days?

About the time of the Jewish Passover, when many thousands of pilgrims were in Jerusalem, the Roman troops were at a high level of readiness. There were soldiers everywhere—not actually in the temple area, but all around it. They would have bloodily suppressed any attempted uprising, just as we see happening now, day after day, in the unholy military situation in the Holy Land. Jesus was acting on his own, and his "cleansing of the temple" was above all a ritual and a symbolic action: "You shall not make my Father's house a house of trade."

The temple is God's house, not the site for an annual fair. That arouses Jesus' zeal and his wrath. What would he say about the behavior of many people in our churches today? How noisy and irreverent it is in some of our churches!

But Jesus does not have only people's outward behavior in mind. This is in fact the expression of an inner attitude. For Jesus, reverence toward the shrine of God's house is a sign that people recognize that they themselves are God's temple. He, Christ, the Son of God, is the dwelling place of God in the form of man. His will is that all men should carry God within themselves and regard their bodies as holy, as temples of God. And it is his will that we set this temple free from the festival of our vanity and our sins. That is the dedication he desires. Celebrating this worldwide makes good sense.

The Gospel of Luke 1:26–38

In the sixth month the angel Gabriel was sent from God to a city of Galilee named Nazareth, to a virgin betrothed to a man whose name was Joseph, of the house of David; and the virgin's name was Mary. And he came to her and said, "Hail, full of grace, the Lord is with you!" But she was greatly troubled at the saying, and considered in her mind what sort of greeting this might be. And the angel said to her, "Do not be afraid, Mary, for you have found favor with God. And behold, you will conceive in your womb and bear a son, and you shall call his name Jesus.

   He will be great, and will be called the Son of the
     Most High;
   and the Lord God will give to him the throne
     of his father David,
   and he will reign over the house of Jacob for ever;
   and of his kingdom there will be no end."

And Mary said to the angel, "How can this be, since I have no husband?" And the angel said to her,

   "The Holy Spirit will come upon you,
   and the power of the Most High will overshadow you;
   therefore the child to be born will be called holy,
   the Son of God.

And behold, your kinswoman Elizabeth in her old age has also conceived a son; and this is the sixth month with her who was called barren. For with God nothing will be impossible." And Mary said, "Behold, I am the handmaid of

the Lord; let it be to me according to your word." And the
angel departed from her.

಄

Conception—A Celebration

Twice in the year, the Church celebrates a feast of conception: on March 25, nine months before Christmas, the conception of Jesus—that is what today's Gospel reading is about—and on December 8, nine months before the Nativity of Mary (September 8), the conception of Mary by her parents, Joachim and Anna. Why celebrate the day of conception? Usually it is only someone's birthday that is celebrated; some people also celebrate their name day. Who knows the day of his own conception?

Have parents happened to talk about it? Has my mother told me one day, in a moment of confidence, how it was that my life began? It is not easy to talk about these things; they are not for discussion in the market place or in the bar with the regulars. And yet that is the moment, for each person, when everything began. At the moment of conception, a new person comes into being. Secretly, we keep the question in our hearts, a question we maybe never dared to ask our parents: What was it like then? Was I welcome? Was the news of my conception the occasion for joy or for horror? Was my conception supposed to have been avoided, and was it then accepted after all, even joyfully, in the end? Would it not be important and helpful for me to know when and how my life began?

Is that not a reason to celebrate? For faith tells me that even if I was unwelcome to my parents, God affirmed me from the beginning, and his affirmation is constant, whatever ups and downs there may be in my life.

Today is a feast of conception; it is called the Feast of the Immaculate Conception. A great deal of misunderstanding is associated with this name. Mary was procreated and conceived by her parents like any human child. The sexual union to which we owe our existence is not something that is "stained", something shameful or sinful. Otherwise, God would not have created people as man and woman, to be there for one another and to pass life on.

What "immaculate" means is, rather, that Mary was "conceived without original sin". The teaching of the Church says that each person, even a newborn child or a child still in his mother's womb, has some lack or some stain attached to him: we are all born into a history of guilt and sin, in which we ourselves become further involved during our lives and to which we contribute through our mistakes. Nobody can free himself from this entanglement by himself. God has to "develop" us, set us free, and disentangle us from this disastrous web. He kept Mary free of it from the moment of her conception onward. For she was meant to be a wholly free and open person, in whom evil could find no foothold.

So when God's plan had reached that stage, Mary was open and ready to become the mother of the Redeemer. What happened to her was hard to bear: becoming pregnant without the child being that of her betrothed. Would he believe that it was, not another man's child, but one conceived by the Holy Spirit? How could that be? Fully trusting in God, Mary said Yes notwithstanding and thus conceived the child who was to set all men free from the chains of guilt.

The conception of Mary, and the conception of Jesus—two feasts. Is not each and every conception a reason for celebration? The beginning of a story without end, because God is faithful!

ASSUMPTION OF MARY

———

The Gospel of Luke 1:39–56

In those days Mary arose and went with haste into the hill country, to a city of Judah, and she entered the house of Zechariah and greeted Elizabeth. And when Elizabeth heard the greeting of Mary, the child leaped in her womb; and Elizabeth was filled with the Holy Spirit and she exclaimed with a loud cry, "Blessed are you among women, and blessed is the fruit of your womb! And why is this granted me, that the mother of my Lord should come to me? For behold, when the voice of your greeting came to my ears, the child in my womb leaped for joy. And blessed is she who believed that there would be a fulfilment of what was spoken to her from the Lord." And Mary said,

"My soul magnifies the Lord,
and my spirit rejoices in God my Savior,
for he has regarded the low estate of his handmaiden.
For behold, henceforth all generations will call me
   blessed;
for he who is mighty has done great things for me,
and holy is his name.
And his mercy is on those who fear him
from generation to generation.
He has shown strength with his arm,
he has scattered the proud in the imagination of their
   hearts,
he has put down the mighty from their thrones,
and exalted those of low degree;
he has filled the hungry with good things,

and the rich he has sent empty away.
He has helped his servant Israel,
in remembrance of his mercy,
as he spoke to our fathers,
to Abraham and to his posterity for ever."
And Mary remained with her about three months, and
returned to her home.

❧

A Blessed Body

At the height of summer, the Church celebrates the Feast of
the Assumption of Mary. Something that in many country
areas is the occasion for traditional celebrations (the blessing
of produce, pilgrimages by water, and so on) is for many
other people mainly a welcome holiday in the hottest time of
the year. But the meaning of this feast, and the reason for the
free holiday, should not be forgotten in all this.

It is a feast of Mary. In many places it is known as "Lady
Day". It has been celebrated for centuries and is firmly
grounded in tradition, yet nonetheless it raises quite a few
questions.

The first and most important arises directly from today's
Gospel reading. It tells of events that have nothing whatever
to do with "the bodily Assumption of Mary into heaven"
(that is the full name of the feast). That, at least, is our first
impression.

A feast with no basis in the Bible? An event not recorded in
Holy Scripture? Is that not a slender basis for such a solemn
celebration? And besides that, it was not until 1950 that Pope
Pius XII solemnly proclaimed, as a dogma of the Church,
that Mary, "having completed the course of her earthly life,

was assumed body and soul into heavenly glory". So, is it a feast with no very sound basis?

Yet may things perhaps be quite different? The fact is that the faithful have particularly loved this feast for centuries. Perhaps the "faithful people" have grasped something here, or sensed it, quite accurately, something not to be found in so many words in the Bible, but that exactly sums up the mystery of this woman. And perhaps it is today's Gospel reading that puts us on the track of that mystery.

It is a simple but gripping scene. Mary has heard from God's messenger, the angel, that her cousin Elizabeth is expecting a child in spite of her advanced age, although she was reckoned to be sterile. Mary herself has conceived. She, too, is expecting a child—not from Joseph, but through God's action.

And now the two pregnant women greet one another, each with the unexpected gift of a child in her womb: one already at six months' gestation, and the other just at the start of her pregnancy.

Then comes the surprise. Elizabeth greets her young relative with a completely unaccustomed solemn greeting. Since then, that greeting has been repeated times without number: "Blessed are you among women, and blessed is the fruit of your womb!"

"Blessed art thou among women . . ."—that is how the Hail Mary takes up Elizabeth's greeting, in somewhat old-fashioned English. Mary is blessed. She is carrying in her womb the child who is going to be a blessing as no other child ever could be: Jesus, the "blessed fruit of your womb". The fact that God's Son has become man in her womb cannot fail to affect her.

"Why is this granted me, that the mother of my Lord should come to me?" asks Elizabeth, in amazement—and she calls Mary, the young woman from Nazareth, "the mother of my Lord". That is the most profound basis for today's feast: Mary is the mother of the Lord, the Redeemer. It was in her case, first of all, that we see what "redemption" means: she was set free from all evil and especially from death. That is why we believe that the blessed body of Mary, too, could not stay in the realm of death. It belonged, not to the grave, but to heaven. What we believe about Mary is what we hope for, for all of us: not the grave, but heaven.

SAINT PETER AND SAINT PAUL

The Gospel of Matthew 16:13–19

Now when Jesus came into the district of Caesarea Philippi, he asked his disciples, "Who do men say that the Son of man is?" And they said, "Some say John the Baptist, others say Elijah, and others Jeremiah or one of the prophets." He said to them, "But who do you say that I am?" Simon Peter replied, "You are the Christ, the Son of the living God." And Jesus answered him, "Blessed are you, Simon Bar-Jona! For flesh and blood has not revealed this to you, but my Father who is in heaven. And I tell you, you are Peter, and on this rock I will build my Church, and the gates of Hades shall not prevail against it. I will give you the keys of the kingdom of heaven, and whatever you bind on earth shall be bound in heaven, and whatever you loose on earth shall be loosed in heaven."

The Human Rock

In the Basilica of Saint Peter in Rome, there is an enormous scriptural quotation running right around the inside of the building, high up beneath the footing of the vault. There we may read, in Latin and in Greek, the words Jesus spoke to Simon Peter in today's Gospel reading. They sound so solemn and weighty that the question arises: Who was the man to whom Jesus said something of such magnitude?

Peter's father, Jonah or John, is mentioned today. His

brother (probably his elder brother) was called Andrew; they came from Bethsaida on the Lake of Gennesaret, and they were fishermen. Peter was married. His mother-in-law is mentioned at one point. Jesus cured her of a high fever. One Christian tradition claims to know about a daughter of Peter, named Petronilla.

Yet it is not Peter's life story that the Gospel is interested in; rather, it is his path to faith. At the beginning of this is Jesus' call to him and his brother, "Follow me, and I will make you become fishers of men!"

Today's scene is a turning point. Who is the person they have now been traveling around with for six months, for whose sake they have left behind their work and their families? They have been through a great deal, have seen how he healed the sick, how marvelous things are happening—for instance, how through the blessing he pronounces, a couple of loaves of bread are multiplied in their hands, as they share them out among thousands of people, so that everyone gets enough to eat.

"Who am I?" That is what Jesus asks them in that out-of-the-way place in northern Galilee, near the source of the Jordan, at Caesarea Philippi. They have heard a lot of what people have been saying and what they think about him. Everyone is agreed that he is a man of God, a prophet. "But you who have been traveling around with me, who am I for you?" This is Peter's hour. Firmly and decidedly, he says, "You are the Messiah, the Son of the living God!" Jesus' reply turned Peter, for all time, into the "human rock". What Simon Peter solemnly proclaimed will remain forever the rock upon which the Church stands firm: Jesus is more than a prophet; he is the Son of God, the Messiah, the Savior.

And Jesus promises that no power in the world, not even that of death, will be able to overcome the Church that is built upon this belief. Jesus also clearly states, however, that he himself will build up this, his Church. She is, not a human achievement, but the work of God himself.

Peter is merely a member of the "ground staff" of the kingdom of heaven. Yet he is the first and the chief "house supervisor". Jesus entrusted him with the keys of his kingdom. Peter does not own the Church, he is merely her caretaker. His task is to open the door to the kingdom of God to as many people as possible, and we hope he will open it for us. He may open it, but we have to enter in ourselves.

The Gospel of Matthew 5:1–12

Seeing the crowds, [Jesus] went up on the mountain, and when he sat down his disciples came to him. And he opened his mouth and taught them, saying:

"Blessed are the poor in spirit, for theirs is the kingdom of heaven.

"Blessed are those who mourn, for they shall be comforted.

"Blessed are the meek, for they shall inherit the earth.

"Blessed are those who hunger and thirst for righteousness, for they shall be satisfied.

"Blessed are the merciful, for they shall obtain mercy.

"Blessed are the pure in heart, for they shall see God.

"Blessed are the peacemakers, for they shall be called sons of God.

"Blessed are those who are persecuted for righteousness' sake, for theirs is the kingdom of heaven.

"Blessed are you when men revile you and persecute you and utter all kinds of evil against you falsely on my account. Rejoice and be glad, for your reward is great in heaven, for so men persecuted the prophets who were before you."

❧

A Heavenly Blueprint

On All Saints' Day we hear the blueprint for all saints. Anyone who lives the way Jesus describes under eight headings will become "blessed". To anyone who takes on Jesus' plan for living, summarized in eight points, Jesus promises that he will be entirely happy forever more.

"Saints" are not only those people whose names are listed in the calendar of saints; they are all those who have well and truly achieved the goal of life and who are therefore "eternally blessed"—or, to put it simply, those "who are in heaven". These people are, so we may hope, infinitely more numerous than all those whose names are set down in the list of saints.

There are certainly a large number. Do they include everyone? Do we all get to heaven? We are permitted to hope so. Jesus talks about a narrow door that everyone has to pass through who wants to achieve the ultimate goal of heavenly bliss. Today he shows us eight ways to get through the narrow gateway to eternal bliss: eight attitudes, situations in life, outlooks on life, that are, so to speak, guaranteed by Jesus to be successful.

In saying this, he is not simply putting everything off to an uncertain future beyond death, which we can of course not examine, as none of us has yet been completely on "the other side". Jesus already calls all those people "blessed" who are following these eight paths. In doing so, he risks having his blueprint checked at any time.

And that is the critical point. For the way that at least half of these eight "rules for happiness" sound, hardly anyone would fancy taking on that kind of program. What is there blissful about being poor or sorrowing, persecuted, mocked, or despised? Those are the very things that no one voluntarily chooses. And Jesus does not dispute that all this means unhappiness and a great deal of pain. Yet he does not turn his gaze away from that pain. There are far more poor people on this earth than people who are well-off. The pain and tears and sorrow are immeasurable. And how many people are suffering through being despised or mocked, through all kinds of torments! To all these people, Jesus is not saying, "Tough luck! You weren't born on the sunny side of the street—you'll just have to grin and bear it!"

On the contrary, Jesus gives the most solemn assurance that all tears will be wiped away, that all misery will come to an end. In doing so, he makes use of a turn of phrase that can be understood only in terms of his Jewish mother tongue. Since the Jews, out of reverence, avoid wherever possible pronouncing the name of God, they prefer to use a circumlocution: "They will be comforted" means "God himself will comfort them." Or, "Theirs is the kingdom of heaven" means "God himself grants them his kingdom and takes them into his blessed fellowship."

Jesus assures the poor and suffering people in this world that God is on their side. They are not forgotten or rejected by him. That is why Jesus calls them "blessed".

Is that not simply putting everything off, even so? No, since Jesus is also saying that all those people who put themselves on the side of the suffering ones, along with God, are blessed. He says that those who are meek, who use no force, and the merciful who do not pass by someone else's suffering, those who make peace, and everyone who is wholeheartedly committed on behalf of justice between men—they are blessed. Jesus calls people with pure and upright hearts blessed because they are really close to God.

Such people make others happy; they comfort them and lighten their troubles. In and through them we can directly experience how God does not overlook any suffering. A little bit of heaven becomes present in this earthly "vale of tears". Is there any better blueprint for happiness?

ALL SOULS

The Gospel of John 11:17–27

Now when Jesus came to Bethany, he found that Lazarus had already been in the tomb four days. Bethany was near Jerusalem, about two miles off, and many of the Jews had come to Martha and Mary to console them concerning their brother. When Martha heard that Jesus was coming, she went and met him, while Mary sat in the house. Martha said to Jesus, "Lord, if you had been here, my brother would not have died. And even now I know that whatever you ask from God, God will give you." Jesus said to her, "Your brother will rise again." Martha said to him, "I know that he will rise again in the resurrection at the last day." Jesus said to her, "I am the resurrection and the life; he who believes in me, though he die, yet shall he live, and whoever lives and believes in me shall never die. Do you believe this?" She said to him, "Yes, Lord; I believe that you are the Christ, the Son of God, he who is coming into the world."

The Hope of All Souls

He ought not to have died. If Jesus had arrived in time, then things would not have gone so far. Why did Lazarus have to die? His sister Martha cannot hide her pain. There is also a reproach in her meeting with Jesus, the friend of these three, who has often stopped at their house when he came to

Jerusalem as a pilgrim. "Why was it this time that you didn't arrive when our brother Lazarus was so ill? This time you could really have helped us. You could have healed him. You've healed so many people, after all. You would certainly have made your friend Lazarus, our brother, well again, and then he wouldn't have died."

How often have such scenes been repeated! "We prayed so hard for mother to get well again. God could have healed her, after all. Why did God take her from us?" How many prayers like that have been prayed! Does God not listen to our cries for help? Is it worth praying at all? Is God not there at the decisive moment, just as Jesus was not with his friends, in those last few days of Lazarus' illness?

Or, do we simply have to come to terms with death? Is it not part of nature, the way the leaves fall in the autumn? That may be so; but what if death snatches away a young person in the springtime of his life? Or if an incurable illness puts an end to someone's life right in the midst of its fullness and creativity?

Sometimes, of course, death comes as a relief from a long period of suffering or sets someone free from a slow descent into torment. In any case, for Martha and Mary their brother's death was not like that. For them, it came far too soon and left behind the painful wounds of parting and separation. In spite of that, Martha does not despair. Her faith gives a great consolation: "I know that my brother will rise again." She believes in eternal life. For her, death is not the end of everything. She even believes in the resurrection of the dead, something that not everyone believed in those days (as, again, nowadays, they do not): that we will rise bodily from the dead and not live on only as souls or spirits. She believes, then, that her brother, who has already been four days in his grave, will not remain there forever. She believes

237

that he, and all other dead people, will be alive in body and soul, as whole persons, "at the last day", at the end of the ages—not alive like our bodies now, but in an immortal body. She believes that with her whole heart. She will meet her brother again one day, not as a pale shadow, but living, in the body. She believes that, even though she cannot exactly imagine it.

And I believe it. This is the faith of the Church; this is what Christians believe. I believe that there will be a real, true new life like that, a happy one, beyond death, one that no death can destroy any more.

Yet I also believe what Martha believed and what so many people have believed since her: that there is not just a life after death and a resurrection of the dead; I believe that even before death, there is a new life. Anyone who believes in Jesus is alive even before death. Jesus says of himself that he is the life. Believing in him brings us to life. Anyone who trusts in him has no need to fear death, whenever it may come. With Jesus, we stand on the side of life, not that of death.